AF446509

JONAH

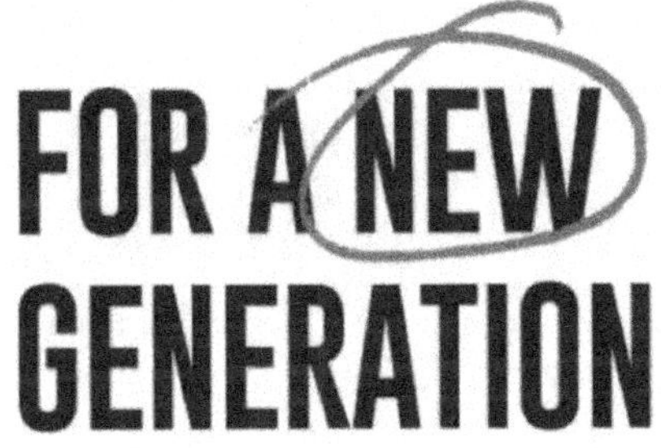

FOR A NEW GENERATION

Ryan Heller

TABLE OF CONTENTS

INTRODUCTION
The Prophet Who Said What We're All Thinking

FORGIVE me. I didn't want to write this book. Don't get me wrong. I love Jonah's story. It's riveting. It's powerful. So why didn't I want to write this book? Because every time I sat down to write, Jonah told me where to look. It's so relevant, it hurts.

Every time I opened my laptop to write about Jonah running away from God, I saw myself. Every time I wrote about Jonah being angry that God was merciful to his enemies, I had to look in the mirror. Every time I wrote about Jonah weeping over a plant while 120,000 innocents perished, I had to admit that I do that thing too.

Jonah is the prophet who said what we're all thinking but are afraid to admit out loud. He's the prophet who got God's call and said, "No thanks." He ran away from where God was calling him. He got angry at God's mercy when God extended mercy to his enemies. He wept over his own comfort more than an entire city's salvation. And somehow God used him anyway. This reluctant, broken prophet was the man God used to bring not one revival, but three. That's the scandal of grace. That's the mystery of revival. God often accomplishes His greatest works through the most unlikely people.

The first revival occurred on a boat in the middle of a storm. Pagan sailors who'd never met the God of Israel ended up fearing Him, offering sacrifices, and making vows. The second revival took place in the darkest, bleakest place imaginable: inside a fish. Jonah finally broke, got honest with God, and experienced resurrection. The third revival is the one we all know about: Nineveh. 120,000 people in the most violent, wicked city on earth repenting in sackcloth and ashes. Three revivals. Three different places. Three different groups of people. But the same relentless God working in and through all of them.

Here's what matters for you: That same God is still in the revival business. He's still pursuing people. Still rescuing rebels. Still using reluctant prophets. And He's getting you ready to be part of what comes next.

That's why this book exists. Not because Jonah was this great, exceptional guy, but because he was exactly like us. Flawed. Stubborn. Angry. Proud. God never gave up on him. Dramatically rescued him. Mercifully recommissioned him. Confrontationally loved him. And He's going to do that for you. The God who wouldn't let Jonah stay in his rebellion won't let you stay in yours. But before God can use you to bring revival to others, He has to bring revival to you first.

Over the next 47 days, you're going to walk through every verse of Jonah's journey. You'll see him run from God's call in chapter 1, pray from the pit in chapter 2, finally obey in chapter 3, then rage at God's mercy in chapter 4. This isn't just information; it's transformation. These 47 days are about getting you revival ready.

The "Live It Out" actions are not some generic set of Christian sounding suggestions. They are specific, challenging, and they vary. Because real change requires movement. Some of them will make you fast. Some of them will make you confess. Some of them will make you squirm. But all of them will move you. They'll move you deeper in relationship with Jesus. They'll move you more like Jesus. And they'll move you toward the kind of person God uses for revival.

Before you get started, you need to know that Jonah was never the hero of this story. Jonah was the preview. Jesus is the better Jonah. The Jesus who didn't run when He was called. The Jesus who went willingly to the depths of hell on our behalf. The Jesus who absorbed the wrath of God so we could experience the compassion of God. Jesus is the ultimate source of all true revival. The one whose death and resurrection ignites true spiritual awakening. Every page of Jonah's story points to the greater rescue mission of the cross.

Are you ready to see yourself in Jonah's rebellion? Are you ready to encounter a God whose mercy makes you uncomfortable because it extends to people you've written off? Are you ready to discover how God brings revival through broken vessels in impossible places? Are you ready to let a relentless God pursue your reluctant heart?

Welcome to the most uncomfortable book in the Bible. Let's find out together what happens when reluctant prophets meet a relentless God…and what happens when you become revival ready.

Is Jonah's Story True?

LET'S just say it: This story sounds more fiction than fact. Could this kind of thing actually happen? Was Jonah really swallowed by a fish, or is this just some ancient fable with a symbolic message?

Here's your strongest piece of evidence: Jesus believed Jonah was real. Matthew 12:40 (ESV) says – *For just as Jonah was three days and three nights in the belly of the great fish...* Jesus wasn't saying, "Here's a cute analogy." He wasn't offering a parable with a moral point. He was saying, "This really happened to Jonah." Jesus accepted Jonah's story as historical fact and built His resurrection prediction on it.

If Jesus (God in the flesh) called Jonah's story literal history, that's good enough for me. Either Jesus was telling the truth about Jonah or Jesus was wrong. And if Jesus was wrong about Jonah, then you have bigger problems than whether a fish story is true.

But what about science? Could this even happen? Are there documented cases of people surviving inside sea creatures? Yes. In 1891, a whaler named James Bartley was reportedly swallowed by a sperm whale and recovered alive hours later.[1] More recently, a whale swallowed a young man who was kayaking. His father had been videoing and the recording shows the big fish spitting out his son after a couple of seconds.[2] A few years earlier in 2021, lobster diver Michael Packard was swallowed by a humpback whale and lived to tell about it. He was trapped inside for over half a minute before the whale surfaced and spit him out.[3] If whales are swallowing people in modern times, why would they not attempt to eat ancient individuals?

Let's be precise: The text never says "whale." It says "great fish." Sperm whales grow up to 60 feet long with throats wide enough to swallow a human whole. Ancient Mediterranean waters had (and still have) massive sea creatures capable of this feat. God "appointed" this particular fish for this particular assignment. This wasn't a marine mishap.

God used part of His creation to achieve His goal. 2 Kings 14: 25 (NLT) mentions *Jonah son of Amittai, the prophet from Gath-hepher* as if he were historical. Jonah was a prophet who ministered during the days of Jeroboam II. This was not some fictitious person created for a teaching story. This was a real prophet who served the Lord and had a known hometown where he ministered.

Why is this important? If Jonah did not actually spend three days in the belly of the fish praying to God, than Jesus' resurrection is not the sign that He claimed it to be. Either the gospel is true or it is an elaborate lie. The miraculous raising of Jesus depends on whether the God that delivered Jonah raised Jesus from the dead. Jonah's three days in the fish is a direct foreshadowing to Jesus' three days in the grave. One miracle proves the other.

Don't let skepticism rob you of belief. If God can create a universe, sustaining a prophet inside a fish for 72 hours is barely a warmup.

Everyone thinks they want to hear from God until God actually speaks. Then suddenly it's complicated. The timing's wrong. The assignment's too hard. The people He's asking you to reach are the ones you've spent years learning to hate. That's where Jonah was when God said, "Go to Nineveh." Instead of saying, "Yes," he said, "Watch me run."

This first chapter is brutal in its honesty. No spiritual platitudes. No "Jonah struggled, but eventually found peace with God's calling." Just straight rebellion. He runs. He pays for the ticket. He boards the ship. He goes down, down, down (physically, emotionally, spiritually) until he's sleeping through a storm that's about to kill everyone around him. When he finally gets exposed, when the lots single him out and the questions corner him, he has to face what he's been avoiding. His disobedience isn't just between him and God; it is affecting everyone in his path.

Welcome to the Book of Jonah. It starts with a prophet who said no. It's about to show you what happens when God refuses to take no for an answer. Buckle up. This isn't a comfortable ride, but it might be exactly what you need.

---

[1] "Man in a Whale's Stomach / Rescue of a Modern Jonah", Yarmouth Mercury (Great Yarmouth: Jarrold & Sons, 22 August 1891), 8.

[2] Andrea Diaz and Ayelen Oliva, "Kayaker Swallowed by Whale Recalls Feeling 'Slimy Texture' in Its Mouth," BBC News, February 14, 2025, https://www.bbc.com/news/articles/cly50k8zypmo. Accessed February 5, 2026.

[3] Doug Fraser, "'I Was Completely inside': Lobster Diver Swallowed by Humpback Whale off Provincetown," Cape Cod Times, June 9, 2022, https://www.capecodtimes.com/story/news/2021/06/11/humpback-whale-catches-michael-packard-lobster-driver-mouth-proviencetown-cape-cod/7653838002/. Accessed February 5, 2026.

CHAPTER 1
The Call and the Run

LET'S get one thing straight. Here's what's about to happen. God is going to call a prophet named Jonah to go and preach to a city called Nineveh. Jonah is going to do something shocking. He's going to say no. Not just no; he's going to run in the exact opposite direction. He'll book a ticket to Tarshish. He'll board a ship. He'll try to outrun God Himself.

But what most people miss when they read this chapter is that Jonah wasn't running from a task; he was running from grace. He knew exactly what would happen if he went and preached to Nineveh. They would repent. God would relent. And the most violent, brutal empire on earth would be shown the same mercy Jonah had received. That's what he couldn't stomach.

Chapter 1 is about the call and the run. It's about a prophet who said no to God and thought he could get away with it. You're going to watch Jonah book his ticket. You're going to watch him board the ship. You're going to watch him sleep through a storm that terrified seasoned sailors. You're going to watch him get exposed by a pagan crew. You're going to watch him confess his God and finally get thrown into the sea.

But pay attention. Every step of Jonah's rebellion becomes someone else's revival. The sailors who never knew the God of Israel end up fearing Him, offering sacrifices, and making vows.

Over the next 17 days, you're going to see yourself in Jonah's running. His excuses. His selective obedience. His attempt to outrun a God who won't be escaped. And you're going to discover something uncomfortable. The same God who pursued Jonah through a storm is pursuing you through these pages.

Let's start at the beginning. Let's watch what happens when God calls and a prophet runs.

DAY 1 ▪ Your Mission, Should You Choose to Accept It

"The word of the LORD came to Jonah son of Amittai."
Jonah 1:1 (NIV)

EVERY *Mission Impossible* movie begins the same way. Brief flashes on the screen of an assignment so dangerous, so completely out of reach that only a secret agent would dare take it on.

Next we get to the now-iconic phrase: "Your mission, should you choose to accept it." God's calling of Jonah follows much the same formula, except for one detail. When *the word of the LORD came to Jonah (NIV)*, this was not advice from headquarters. This was the Creator of the universe speaking to one man at one point in time for one purpose. No props. No support crew. Just a prophet with a ludicrous assignment.

Here's the thing. In the movies, Ethan Hunt always says yes. He loves impossible odds. But Jonah? He runs. And yet the call of God stands. The mission does not self-destruct in five seconds. It pursues.

Notice how simple this verse comes across. No smoke and flames. No voice from the sky. Just six words in Hebrew that would change everything: *The word of the LORD came (NIV)*. This is how calling often works. Not with fireworks, but with clarity. A conviction that lands on your spirit. A door that swings wide open. A burden that won't lift. A conversation that reroutes your path.

When God calls, He reveals a unique assignment designed specifically for you. He doesn't send you on missions where failure is expected. He supplies what He calls for. Your credentials, your readiness, your comfort level? Those aren't His main criteria. His strength working through your weakness is the whole point.

Jonah wasn't particularly courageous. He didn't relish Nineveh. He had hard questions about God's mercy extending to Israel's enemies. And yet the word came to him anyway. God called the reluctant prophet to the impossible mission.

The same God is calling today. Perhaps not audibly, but through His Word, through circumstances, through the persistent tugging of the Holy Spirit. He's calling ordinary people to extraordinary obedience. The question isn't whether you're qualified. The question is whether you'll respond.

Your mission probably won't involve disarming nuclear devices. It might be a conversation you've been avoiding, a calling you've been resisting, a step of faith that terrifies you. God specializes in impossible missions that become testimonies of His faithfulness when you simply say yes.

Live It Out:

- **Accept the briefing.** Spend five minutes in silence asking God, "What assignment have I been running from?" Write down whatever comes to mind.

- **Declassify your fears.** Write down the three biggest reasons you've avoided God's call. Bring each one to Him in prayer, asking Him to replace your excuses with His empowerment.

- **Study the intel.** Read Jonah 1 today. Circle every action verb and notice how both Jonah and God are constantly moving. Ask yourself, "Am I moving toward my assignment or away from it?"

DAY 2 ▪ Get Up and Go

"Get up! Go to the great city of Nineveh and preach against it because their evil has come up before me." Jonah 1:2 (CSB)

GOD didn't send Jonah to a place. He sent him to people. Nineveh was not a coordinate on a map, not a dangerous place to send a hot-shot missionary on an impossible errand. Nineveh was 120,000 people who couldn't tell their right hand from their left. They were flesh and blood. People made in God's image. People destined for destruction. People who desperately needed to hear about the mercy of God.

When God says, "Get up and go," He's not sending you on an errand. He's inviting you into the greatest work in the universe: joining His rescue mission for lost humanity. Every person you pass on the street, meet at work, or connect with on social media is someone Jesus died for. Every frustrating relationship is an opportunity for the gospel to break through. Every enemy is a potential worshiper waiting to hear that God's mercy is so big that it even reaches them.

Who is your Nineveh? Not what task are you avoiding, but who are the people God is calling you to reach? It might be the coworker everyone has written off. It might be the family member whose lifestyle makes you uncomfortable. It might be the neighbor you've been avoiding because you don't know what to say. It might be the person whose politics, past, or patterns have convinced you they're beyond hope.

Jonah ran because he knew this truth: God's heart is for people we'd sometimes rather see judged than saved. He wasn't afraid Nineveh would reject the message. He was terrified they'd receive it. And that's exactly what happened. When Jonah finally obeyed, the most violent, godless city in the ancient world experienced the greatest revival in the Old Testament. Every single person, from the king to the commoners, turned to God.

That's the scandal of the gospel. Jesus didn't come for people who had it all together. He came for Nineveh. He came for sinners, enemies, and rebels. He died for people who hated Him so they could become people who worship Him. And now He sends us to tell them.

Revival doesn't start with perfect messengers. It starts with obedient ones. Jonah was bitter, reluctant, and full of prejudice, yet God used his eight-word sermon to save an entire empire. Your willingness matters more than your eloquence. Your obedience matters more than your credentials.

Stop waiting for the right words or the right moment. Stop making excuses about why someone else is better qualified. Get up. Go to the people God has placed in your path. Tell them about the Jesus who pursued you when you were running, who rescued you when you were drowning, who gave you mercy you didn't deserve.

Your Nineveh isn't a task to complete. It's a person to reach. And revival is waiting on the other side of your obedience.

Live It Out:

- **Pray by name.** Write down three people who seem furthest from God. Pray specifically for each of them every day this week. Ask God to prepare their hearts and give you an opportunity to speak.
- **Have the conversation.** Text or call one person this week and say, "Can I tell you what Jesus has done in my life?" Then actually tell them.
- **Go where they are**. Put yourself in one place this week where lost people gather. Not to judge them but to reach them. Let them see Jesus in you before you say a word about Him.

DAY 3 ▪ Wrong Way: Do Not Enter

But Jonah got up to flee to Tarshish from the LORD's presence. He went down to Joppa and found a ship going to Tarshish. He paid the fare and went down into it to go with them to Tarshish from the LORD's presence.   Jonah 1:3 (CSB)

JONAH didn't merely disobey God's instruction. He deliberately ran from God's presence. God told him to head east to Nineveh. Jonah boarded a ship going west to Tarshish. When Jonah saw the "Do Not Enter" sign, he drove on the highway ramp.

Notice how the CSB puts it: *from the LORD's presence* is repeated twice in this verse. Jonah was running from a pursuing God. He was trying to escape God Himself. He thought if he could put enough distance between himself and the calling, maybe God would forget about him or find someone else. But you can't outrun omnipresence.

Jonah paid a fare, boarded a ship, went down into it. Notice all the downward movement. Every "Wrong Way" sign he ignored took him further down. Running from God never takes you up. It only takes you down.

The irony is insane. Jonah worked harder to run from God than he would have if he'd just obeyed in the first place. He traveled to Joppa. Researched ships. Paid for a ticket, which wasn't cheap. Sailed across the Mediterranean. All to avoid a conversation he knew he needed to have.

Running from God is the most exhausting work you'll ever do. It drains you physically. Your body carries the weight of rebellion. It depletes you emotionally. You're constantly looking over your shoulder. It bankrupts you spiritually. Every step away from God's will is a step toward emptiness. The money spent on distractions. The energy wasted on avoidance. The relationships strained by your absence. The opportunities missed while you're sailing the wrong direction. Running costs more than obedience ever would.

What is your Tarshish? Jonah's assignment was not simply Nineveh. Jonah's assignment was to deliver God's message to the people who needed to hear it. That's your assignment too. Every believer is an advocate. You're not just called to be an evangelist if you're a pastor, a missionary, or a youth pastor. You're called to be a truth-teller. Period.

Maybe you're avoiding conversations with coworkers who don't know Jesus. Maybe you're avoiding that neighbor, that family member, that friend that you know needs to hear about God's love. Maybe you've been convincing yourself that evangelism is someone else's job, that you're not equipped, that you're too uncomfortable, that you'll do it "someday." You know the people God has placed in your path and you feel the nudge. You've been working really hard to convince yourself it's easier to stay silent.

Running is costly. The energy you're spending to avoid God's will could have already accomplished it. The money you're investing in distractions could have funded your obedience. The time you're wasting in resistance could have brought breakthrough. Every day you run is another day you're not living in your purpose.

You can run to Tarshish, but God's presence is everywhere and His calling doesn't expire just because you ignore it. Eventually you'll have to land. The question is, how much will it cost you before you do?

Live It Out:

- **Cancel your flight to Tarshish.** Delete one app, unsubscribe from one distraction, or end one habit you've been using to avoid God's voice. Your 30-day digital detox starts now.

- **Create a "cost of running" invoice.** Line by line, write down what avoiding God has cost you (peace, time, money, relationships, opportunities). Total it up. Then pray over it and ask God to redeem what you've lost by finally obeying.

- **Go down, then get up.** The text says Jonah "went down" three times. Identify three areas where running from God has taken you downward (relationship, finances, mental health, spiritual life). For each one, take one specific upward action this week—a hard conversation, a budget adjustment, a return to prayer.

DAY 4 ■ Divine Disruption

*But the LORD hurled a powerful wind over the sea, causing a
violent storm that threatened to break the ship apart.*
Jonah 1:4 (NLT)

YOUR car breaks down. Your job falls through. A
relationship implodes. All in the same week. It feels like
the universe is against you. That's what happened to
Jonah and everyone on his ship. God sent a storm so
fierce that experienced sailors who'd spent their entire
lives on the water feared for their lives. Jonah thought
he could outrun his calling. Instead, he got caught in a
divine disruption. This was God's way of stopping him
before he went off the deep end.

The storm wasn't random. It was divine intervention.
God pursued Jonah with a hurricane because sometimes
love looks like disruption. When we run from God, He
doesn't just let us go. He loves us too much to leave us
lost at sea. The storm was severe, but it was also mercy.
God was giving Jonah a chance to turn around before he
got too far gone. The ship *threatened to break (NLT)*, which
is exactly what happens when we persist in disobedience.
Our lives start to fracture under the weight of choices
we were never meant to carry.

Sometimes the storm in your life isn't random. It's
not fate. It's not the universe working against you.
Sometimes it's God interrupting your plans because He
loves you. I've been there. There were jobs I knew I was
more than qualified for, with more experience and a
stronger résumé, and still I didn't get them. I was angry
and confused, but, looking back, God was in it all. I
couldn't see it at the time, but God needed me
elsewhere.

Before you blame God or call yourself unlucky, stop and ask, "Was I running from something He wanted me to do? Was I heading somewhere I didn't belong?" The storm might not be punishment; it might be rescue. That interruption you're resenting could be the most loving thing God has done for you all year.

But divine disruption has another side. Jonah's storm affected everyone around him. The sailors didn't sign up for his rebellion, but they were caught in it. When we run from God, we rarely run alone. Our choices ripple out and touch the people closest to us. Family. Friends. Coworkers. Roommates. Obedience isn't just about you. It's about everyone connected to your calling.

The good news? Storms sent by God always have a purpose. They're meant to turn you around, not destroy you. Even when you're caught in divine disruption, God is still present, still pursuing, still loving you enough to disrupt your plans before they ruin your life.

Live It Out:

- **Tell the truth about the hurricane**. If you feel like your life is falling apart, as God point blank, "Is there disobedience fueling this hurricane?" Journal whatever pops in your head—no filter.

- **Apologize to your shipmates.** Who got caught in the storm you created with your rebellion? Text or leave them a voice note that says, "I'm sorry my decisions impacted you. This is how I will be different."

- **Rename the storm.** Print this out and place it where you will see it every day: Storms are not punishment. They're pursuit. God loves me enough to disrupt me."

DAY 5 ▪ Numb and Number

The sailors were afraid, and each cried out to his own god. And they threw the ship's cargo into the sea to lighten the load. But Jonah had gone down to the lowest part of the vessel, where he lay down and fell into a deep sleep.   Jonah 1:5 (BSB)

IMAGINE a category 5 hurricane is tearing this ship apart. Pagan sailors are yelling prayers to every god they can think of. Cargo is being tossed overboard to keep the ship from sinking. But Jonah? He's asleep. Knocked out. While everyone else is scrambling to stay alive, Jonah is completely checked out.

How do you sleep through a storm like that? By exhausting yourself trying to run from God. Jonah was physically, emotionally, and spiritually exhausted. Running from your calling sucks everything out of you. He went down to the lowest part of the ship (see the downward motion again?) and passed out, completely disconnected from the storm he brought on. This is the worst-case scenario of avoidance. When life gets too uncomfortable, when consequences become too overwhelming, sometimes we just shut down.

That's the contrast in this verse. Pagan sailors who don't even know the true God are crying out to their gods, trying everything they can to survive. They're praying. They're problem-solving. They're throwing cargo overboard. They're spiritually engaged, physically active, emotionally present. Meanwhile, God's prophet is out cold. The people who don't know God are more spiritually alive in that moment than the guy who's supposed to be His spokesperson.

Being numb and number isn't rest; it's resignation. It's giving up without officially quitting. It's being physically present but emotionally and spiritually absent. God won't let you stay there. He loves you too much to let you sleep through the storm.

When you run from your calling, you become less alive, less aware, less present. You lose the very thing that makes you who you are. The sailors are fighting for life while Jonah has checked out of his own story. Running from God doesn't only take you to the wrong place; it makes you numb to everything that matters.

Jonah's running hard. But here's what he doesn't know yet: You can't outrun God. And sometimes the thing you're running from is actually God's rescue plan.

Live It Out:
- **The Cargo Audit:** List what you're "throwing overboard" to fix your problems (overtime hours, forced relationships, security expenditures, image management). Next to each, write what you fear will happen if you stop trying to control it. Pray, "God, I've been trying to save myself with _____. I'm putting this in your hands." Pick one thing to stop forcing this week.
- **The Advice Diet**: Pick one problem you're facing. For the next 3 days, ask no one for advice. No social media polls. No group text problem solving. No "what would you do?" coffee dates. Just you and God. Pray about it daily. Journal what He reveals to you. See if you can trust God's voice before filling up on everyone else's opinions.
- **The DIY Detox:** Identify one problem where you've been micromanaging God's solution. Commit to a 24-hour "DIY detox." No problem solving, no strategizing, no fixing. Just pray, "God, I'm done trying to be my own savior. Show me

what you want to do here." Write down any impressions, ideas, or peace that comes. God often speaks when we stop shouting our own solutions at Him.

Day 6 ▪ The Wake-Up Call

The captain approached him and said, "What are you doing sound asleep? Get up! Call on your god. Maybe this god will consider us, and we won't perish." Jonah 1:6 (CSB)

Sometimes God uses the most unexpected people to wake us up. In Jonah's case it was a pagan ship captain who had no personal relationship with the God of Israel. While Jonah was sleeping through the storm he caused, the captain found him and basically said, "What is wrong with you? Get up and pray!" This was Jonah's wake-up call. And it came from the last person he expected.

It's ironic and deeply convicting. The prophet of God had to be called out by someone who didn't even know God personally. That's embarrassing. But it's also exactly what Jonah needed.

The captain's words are simple but piercing. *"What are you doing sound asleep? Get up!" (CSB)* It's almost identical to God's original command back in verse 2. When we ignore God's first call, He'll send a second messenger. Sometimes it's a friend who loves you enough to tell you the truth you don't want to hear. Sometimes it's a consequence that forces you to pay attention. Sometimes it's a stranger who has more spiritual awareness in that moment than you do. God will use anyone and anything to reach you when you're running.

Wake-up calls are hard. No one enjoys having their sleep interrupted by someone telling them they need to change. But it's also grace. The captain could have let Jonah sleep. He could have thrown him overboard without waking him, assuming Jonah was dead weight. But the captain woke him up and gave him a chance to pray, a chance to make it right. When you're called out, it's not always an attack. Sometimes it's an invitation to wake up to your purpose and responsibility, to stop sleeping and start facing the crisis you've created.

God is not giving up on you. Even when you've checked out, He's still working to wake you up. The question is whether you'll receive the wake-up call or hit snooze again.

Live It Out:

- **Don't hit snooze on truth.** If someone called you out recently, sit with it for 10 minutes. Journal this: "God, is there truth in what they said that I've been avoiding?"
- **Check your spiritual pride.** Stop assuming you're the most spiritually aware person in the room. Listen to what God is saying and respond accordingly.
- **Eliminate the escape routes.** Tonight, turn off your phone. No music. No friends. No apps. Just you and God in prayer.

DAY 7 ▪ There Is No Such Thing as Luck

"Come on!" the sailors said to each other. "Let's cast lots. Then we'll know who is to blame for this trouble we're in." So they cast lots, and the lot singled out Jonah.   Jonah 1:7 (CSB)

IF you've scrolled social media lately, you've seen friends checking their horoscope before a date, coworkers "manifesting" a promotion, others posting that the universe has a plan. We've invented a spiritual system that worships cosmic randomness but won't accept a God who's actually in control. The sailors weren't that different. They cast lots. But they didn't realize that fate wasn't in charge…God was.

Casting lots was the ancient world's way of letting chance determine an outcome. Draw straws, roll dice, pull names from a bag—trust whatever happens was meant to be. The sailors used this method to find who caused the storm. They weren't being superstitious; this was their earnest attempt to get a sign from God. And it worked. Not because the lots had power, but because God directed them.

The lot singled out Jonah (CSB). That phrase is packed with meaning. The lots didn't randomly fall on Jonah by mistake. God caused them to. Proverbs 16:33 says it clearly: *The lot is cast into the lap, but its every decision is from the* LORD *(NIV).* What looks like chance to us is actually God's sovereignty at work. The sailors thought they were asking fate. They were actually asking the God of the universe, and He responded.

This shatters our modern fascination with luck and randomness. We say, "I just happened to…" or "What are the odds…" or "It's just a coincidence…" as if God's not paying attention. As if your life is a cosmic slot machine and you're just hoping the right symbols line up. But there's no such thing as luck in God's economy. There's providence. There's sovereignty. There's a God intimately involved in every detail, directing outcomes we think are random.

Think of the "coincidences" in your life. The job offer that came exactly when you needed it. The friend who texted precisely when you were at your lowest. The delay that saved you from danger you didn't even know was coming. That wasn't luck. That wasn't the universe. That was God actively, intentionally, sovereignly orchestrating your life.

The sailors cast lots and Jonah got exposed. Not by accident, but by design. God was in control the whole time. And He still is. Your mercury isn't in retrograde. Your stars aren't misaligned. Your karma isn't bad. God is sovereign, and He's writing a story you can't see yet. Stop trusting randomness. Start trusting Him.

Live It Out:

- **Delete all apps or unfollow accounts** that promote astrology, manifesting, or "universe" theology. Replace it with biblical teaching or a Bible app.
- **Confess God's authority.** Before you make any decision this week (large or small), pause and pray specifically, "God, I know you are sovereign over the outcome. Direct me." Get in the habit of confessing His control before the outcome.
- **Memorize one Bible verse** about God's sovereignty over "random" events (Proverbs 16:33, Acts 17:26, Matthew 10:29-31). Next time you feel anxious about the future, speak that truth instead of wishing for "good luck."

DAY 8 ▪ Live Your Truth

So they asked him, "Tell us, who is responsible for making all this trouble for us? What kind of work do you do? Where do you come from? What is your country? From what people are you?"
Jonah 1:8 (NIV)

HAVE you ever found yourself in a moment where someone asks you a question, and you know as soon as you answer that everything is going to change? Jonah found himself in such a moment. The sailors were serious. The storm was intensifying. The lot had convicted Jonah. Now they wanted answers. Four questions. Direct. To the point. Who are you? What do you do? Where are you from? What's your deal?

These were not casual inquiries. These were not idle questions at a professional mixer. These were accountability questions. The kind of questions that cut through niceties, straight to reality. The sailors wanted answers because their lives were on the line. The storm was of God and someone on this ship was responsible. Jonah could not deflect, joke his way out, dodge and weave, nor could he be vague and carry on. He was on the horns of truth and the only path forward was brutal honesty.

You hear people talk about "living your truth" all the time, but that phrase usually just means doing whatever you want or following your feelings wherever they lead. Real truth is different. It's not about feelings. It's not about what you like or don't like. It's about your actual vocation. Your actual identity in God. Your willingness to confess reality even when it costs you something.

It sounds freeing until you realize it's often just a code word for living your lies. The sailors weren't asking

Jonah to share his feelings about his life's journey. They were asking him for truth. The kind of truth that lays bare who you really are and not who you want people to think you are.

Questions like these are not meant to corner you. They're meant to set you free. Because when you answer them honestly, when you stop running from who you are, you can finally stop pretending and start living the life God made for you. When you stop dodging reality, God can start restoring the real you.

Healing starts when you trade excuses for honesty, when you choose confession over comfort. The questions are not going to go away. Your only choice is if you'll answer them now or run until the storm forces you to.

Live It Out:

- **Create a truth timeline.** Draw a line representing your life. Mark moments when you dodged hard questions. Pick one. Go back and answer it now, even if it's years overdue.

- **Swap places with Jonah.** Get alone and ask the sailors' questions in Jonah 1:8. What is your business? Where are you from? What is your country? What people are you from? Answer these questions spiritually, not literally. Who are you at your core? What is God calling you to do? Are you running or walking in obedience to that call? Write down honest answers. If you are running, name what you are running from. Then stop.

- **Write your bio as God would.** If God introduced you to the sailors, what would He say about your calling, your origin, your purpose? Write it from His perspective.

DAY 9 ▪ The Identity Gap

Jonah answered, "I am a Hebrew, and I worship the LORD, the God of heaven, who made the sea and the land."
Jonah 1:9 (NLT)

IDENTITY is everything. Who you think you are shapes how you make decisions, how you show up in the world, who you date, where you work, what you value, and what you're willing to sacrifice. After a series of more leading questions, Jonah finally has an answer. Who am I? His answer is interesting. *"I am a Hebrew, and I worship the* LORD, *the God of heaven, who made the sea and the land"* (NLT). In one sentence, he claimed his ethnicity, his faith, his God. But the tension lives in the identity gap between his words and his actions.

Jonah's theology is spot on. He worships the Lord. The Lord is the Creator of all. The Lord is the God of the sea, the object of Jonah's escape. There's irony dripping from this text. How can you say you worship the God who made the sea and then use the sea to run from God? How can you claim to worship the God of the heavens, yet hide in the lowest part of a ship? This is the identity gap in full display. Jonah knew the right words, the right confession, the right doctrine. He knew what he should be, he just wasn't acting like it.

I grew up in the home of Christian parents, but it wasn't until college that my faith began to gel. I had heard the gospel hundreds of times, but one day it just clicked. I'm God's child. In that moment I, like Jonah, connected my faith with my identity. The identity gap closed when belief became action. Your identity is revealed in your actions, not just your answers to theological questions.

If you are in Christ, your identity isn't rooted in ethnicity, achievements, or even our religious activity. It's rooted in Christ. You are loved, forgiven, chosen, and adopted, not because of what you've done but because of what He's accomplished. That's the identity that should shape every move you make. Your identity in Christ isn't just a theological truth to memorize. It's a lived reality that transforms how you move through the world.

But there's hope in Jonah's story. Even in the middle of his rebellion, he still claimed his identity. He didn't lie, didn't pretend to be someone else, or make up a fake story to protect himself. He owned who he was even though his behavior hadn't caught up yet. That's the first step toward change. You have to name who you are before you can become who you're meant to be.

When you remember who you belong to, your choices start to shift. The decisions get clearer. The distractions lose their power. Close the identity gap by letting your identity in Christ shape how you talk, lead, serve, and respond when life tests your integrity.

Live It Out:

- **Own your identity.** In one or two sentences, describe who you are in Christ. Be honest about where you are, not just where you want to be. Read it out loud daily this week.

- **Test where you're finding value.** Write down three things you're tempted to find your worth in (job, performance, other's approval). Cross them out. Next to each one, write a truth about your identity in Christ (chosen, forgiven, adopted, beloved). Which list are you actually living from?

- **Name the distraction.** Pick one thing that consistently has power over you (relationship, habit, screen time, approval). Ask yourself, "Does this fit who I belong to?" If not, take one step this week to let it go.

DAY 10 • The Group Chat Finds Out

Then the men were seized by a great fear and said to him, "What have you done?" The men knew he was fleeing from the LORD's presence because he had told them. Jonah 1:10 (CSB)

YOU know that nightmare-type stomachache when you realize everyone knows your little secret? That's what happened to Jonah. Everyone in the group chat finds out. Sailors were stumped on the storm. They were looking for answers. But once Jonah explained who he was and what he'd done, everything clicked. They were *seized by a great fear* and asked the question we all dread, *"What have you done?" (CSB)*.

Their fear wasn't just about the storm anymore. It had shifted to something deeper. They were dealing with the God of creation, the One who made the sea and the land. And His runaway prophet had dragged them into the mess. They asked what he had done, not because they didn't know. Jonah had already told them he was fleeing from the Lord's presence. They asked because they couldn't believe someone would be foolish enough to run from a God that powerful. It was shock. Fear. Probably some anger too. They were risking their lives because one man decided to disobey.

People might be more afraid of your God than you are. The sailors feared the Lord after hearing Jonah's story. They understood the gravity of who they were dealing with. They got it immediately. Meanwhile Jonah had been treating God like someone he could ignore, negotiate with, avoid. He'd lost his reverence, his awe, his healthy fear of the Lord.

Sometimes unbelievers have more reverence for God than believers do. That should wake us up and make us reconsider how casually we've been treating the Creator of the universe.

Live It Out:

- **Write, "What have you done?" on a sticky note.** Put it on your bathroom mirror. Every time you see it this week, answer it honestly before God. Let the question drive you to run to God for His forgiveness and purpose for your life.
- **Find one person who fears God more than you do right now.** Ask them to pray for you. Tell them, "I've been treating God casually. Help me get my reverence back."
- **Let God be big again.** Spend 10 minutes this week reading Psalm 19, 29, or 104 out loud. Let the weight of who God is crush your casual approach to Him.

DAY 11 ▪ Coming Clean

Now the sea was growing worse and worse, so they said to Jonah, "What must we do to you to calm this sea for us?"
Jonah 1:11 (BSB)

THE check engine light has been on for three months. You drive past mechanics all the time, convincing yourself it's probably nothing. Maybe it'll just go away on its own. Then one day your car starts shaking, smoke comes from the hood, and you pull over on the side of the highway to call a tow truck. The mechanic pops the hood and asks, "How long has this been going on?" You have to own it. You have to say, "I've known something was wrong with this for months." That's coming clean. Finally admitting what everyone already knew was broken.

The sailors had been throwing cargo, praying to their gods, fighting the storm with everything they had. Then they turned to Jonah and asked straight up, "What should we do to you?" There's a moment in every crisis when someone finally asks the question everyone's been dancing around. The sailors had tried everything and nothing was working. So they turned to Jonah with brutal honesty about what needed to happen next.

Notice they didn't ask, "What should we do about this situation?" They asked, "What should we do to you?" They knew Jonah was the problem. The lot had exposed him. His confession had confirmed it. Now they needed him to tell them how to fix what he'd broken. That's accountability at its rawest. When the people affected by your choices look you in the eye and say, "You caused this. Now what?"

It's powerful when you stop being a victim of circumstances and start being honest about your role in creating them. Jonah had to face the truth. He was the problem. Until he owned that, nothing would change. No amount of cargo tossing would help. No amount of rowing would work. The storm would keep raging until Jonah stopped deflecting and started taking responsibility.

Honesty isn't weakness. It's worship. God can't heal what we hide, but He rushes toward what we reveal. The same storm that felt like punishment may actually be His mercy pushing you toward freedom. When you finally tell the truth, you stop sinking and start finding grace in the waves.

The sea was getting worse and worse. Sometimes that's what it takes. Sometimes God lets the pressure build until honesty becomes the only option left. The lots exposed Jonah. But exposure isn't the end; it's the beginning of confession. Hold onto that thought. We're about to see Jonah get tossed overboard. And then we're going to see that sometimes going down is the only way up.

Live It Out:

- **Fix what you've been ignoring.** Just like that check engine light, identify one warning sign in your life you've been driving past for months. Now go obey what God has told you to do in the first place.

- **Label your role in the chaos.** Jot down one instance where you've been playing the victim. Fill in this sentence honestly: "The storm is raging because I…" Say what you wrote to God first, then to one person you trust.

- **End the deflection cycle.** Name one arena where you've been blaming circumstances, other people, or timing for something you caused or contributed to. This week, tell someone the whole truth about your role in it.

Day 12 ▪ The Swap

"Pick me up and throw me into the sea," he replied, "and it will become calm. I know that it is my fault that this great storm has come upon you." Jonah 1:12 (NIV)

WILD, right? Jonah just told a group of sailors to throw him into a raging sea so they could live. He finally got it. His rebellion caused the storm. His disobedience put innocent people in danger. And the only way to stop it was for him to take the fall. One life for many. Sound familiar?

This is substitution at its core. Jonah wasn't saying, "Hey, maybe if we all work together we can figure this out." He was saying, "I'm the problem and I need to be removed for you to survive." That's the language of exchange, of someone trading places with the guilty to save the innocent. That's exactly what Jesus did on the cross. He took the punishment we deserved so we could be saved from the storm of God's judgment.

Obviously, Jonah isn't Jesus. He's a flawed, rebellious prophet who caused his own crisis. But even in his mess, God was previewing the greatest swap in history. Jonah offered himself to save sailors who didn't deserve to die. Jesus offered Himself to save humanity who did deserve to die. Jonah's swap bought them time. Jesus' swap bought us eternity.

The difference? Jonah was guilty taking the consequences of his own sin. Jesus was innocent taking the consequences of ours. That's the scandal of the gospel. The sinless one swapped places with the sinful ones. The righteous died for the unrighteous. God's wrath that should have fallen on us fell on Him instead. This is the heart of Christianity. Not self-improvement.

Not religious performance. But substitution. Someone else paying the price you owe.

What are the storms in your life right now? The chaos. The anxiety. The relational fractures. The financial stress. What would it look like to stop trying to save yourself and instead surrender to what God is asking? Maybe He's asking you to let go of control. Maybe He's asking you to sacrifice something you've been clinging to. Maybe He's asking you to take full responsibility for something you've been blaming others for.

The swap isn't about giving up. It's about trusting that God has a plan even when the plan looks difficult. Jonah was about to learn that the hard way.

Live It Out:

- **Identify one area where you need to take full responsibility** instead of making excuses. Own it completely today.
- **Ask yourself, "What am I clinging to** that God might be asking me to throw overboard?" Write it down. Then let it go.
- **Accept Jesus as your substitute.** He took the storm you deserved so you could have peace with God. If you've already received this gift, thank Him for being your substitute and living proof that the greatest swap in history is real.

DAY 13 · Stop Fighting It

Instead, the sailors rowed even harder to get the ship to the land. But the stormy sea was too violent for them, and they couldn't make it.   Jonah 1:13 (NLT)

HAVE you ever seen someone try to go backwards through a revolving door? They plant their feet, push against the direction it's designed to move, and create chaos for everyone else trying to get through. The door's not going to reverse for you. It's built to go one way.

These sailors had guts. Jonah just told them to throw him overboard. It was the obvious solution. The only solution. But they didn't want to do it. So they rowed. They rowed hard. They gave it everything they had trying to save Jonah and save themselves. But the sea kept raging. Rowing against the flow never works when God is the one controlling the current.

Every stroke took them further from peace. Every attempt to find their own solution delayed the calm they desperately needed. The answer was right there. Jonah had told them what to do. But they wanted a different answer. A less costly answer. An answer that didn't require them to do something that felt wrong even though it was right.

How much longer are you going to row? How much more energy are you going to waste trying to avoid what God has already shown you? The sea is becoming more violent. Your strength is running out.

Live It Out:

- **Ask yourself, "Am I rowing uphill?"** Name one area where you've been working hard but seeing no results. Ask God if you're rowing against His will.
- **Pick a specific area to increase your trust in the Lord.** Stop one thing you've been striving to control. Let it go.
- **Make it your goal to stop forcing a solution for at least 24 hours.** Every time you're tempted, pray instead.

DAY 14 ▪ Root Access

So they called to the LORD, *"Please,* LORD, *don't let us perish for this man's life, or count innocent blood to our account. For you,* LORD, *have done as you have pleased." Jonah 1:14 (CSB)*

I'M not a tech guy, but I do know the technical term "root access." Root access on a computer means unfettered access to everything in the system. A regular user can open applications, save files, change preferences. A root user can delete critical system files, turn off protections, recode programs. They have permission to alter what regular users cannot.

The sailors had normal user access. When the storm hit, their gods didn't have root access to override it. All they could do was run user-level commands in a panic: throw cargo, adjust sails, pray harder. Nothing worked because their gods had no root access to the system God created. Then they called on THE God, the One who coded the entire system, who has Administrator privileges over wind and waves. Everything changed.

This is a complete 180. Back in verse 5, these sailors were crying out to their *gods* (plural, lowercase). Now they're praying to the LORD (singular, uppercase). They moved from basic user account to THE System Administrator. This is conversion happening in real time. This is what revival looks like.

Sometimes people furthest from God get it faster than those who've been around church their whole lives. Why? They don't have the luxury of religious familiarity. No backup plan. When they meet the living God who actually has root access to their situation, they know it. And they respond immediately.

When was the last time you prayed like these sailors? Not a routine prayer. Not a grocery list. But a desperate, humble cry to THE God who has root access to all things, including your storm? Prayer upgrade happens when you stop treating God like one option and start recognizing Him as your only hope. He is the only one with full permissions to override what you can't change.

Live It Out:

- **Identify how familiar you have become with God.** Ask yourself, "Do I pray to God as if He were one option among many, or as if He were THE only Admin with root access?" If you have been operating as though God was merely a user level setting opposed to the System Developer, then repent of it. Revival begins when religious rituals are exchanged for desperate awareness of who God is.

- **Grant full permissions.** List three areas of your life where you've been giving God limited user-level access. Write "administrator privileges granted to God today" next to each one. Sign and date it.
- **Pray the sailors' prayer in your crisis.** Take their exact words from verse 14 and insert your situation: "Please, Lord, don't let me perish for ______. For you, Lord, have done as you have pleased." Pray it out loud three times this week.

DAY 15 ▪ Stop Raging

Then they picked up Jonah and threw him into the sea, and the sea stopped its raging.   Jonah 1:15 (CSB)

I WAS on a plane recently and behind me a toddler was screaming horribly. I tried ignoring it, I tried drowning the sound with headphones, but nothing worked. I was sitting there with clenched jaw, completely on edge. Suddenly the kid fell asleep and the cabin went silent. Literally everyone around me sighed at once.

That's what the sailors felt. For hours they'd been rowing against the storm, dumping cargo, running out of options. Then they did the one thing they hadn't: they obeyed God and threw Jonah into the sea. Instantly the raging stopped. One second chaos. Next second calm. That's what obedience does.

One second the sea was a war zone. The next second it was smooth as glass. They threw Jonah overboard and immediately the sea stopped raging. When you finally do what God's been asking, peace shows up faster than you thought possible.

The sailors didn't want to throw Jonah overboard. They obeyed reluctantly. But when they finally did what God required, peace came instantly. How many storms are you enduring that one act of obedience could end? How many relationships could find peace if you'd just have that conversation? How many anxieties could calm if you'd just surrender that control? How much drama could end if you'd just do what God's been asking?

Think about it. The sailors tried everything else first. Rowing. Praying to their gods. Throwing cargo. All the effort in the world couldn't calm what only obedience could settle. Sometimes we exhaust ourselves trying every solution except the one God has already given us.

Obedience isn't always easy, but it's always worth it. Sometimes the peace you've been praying for is one decision away.

Live It Out:

- **Do the thing God has been asking you to do.** Schedule it right now. Put it on your calendar.
- **Notice where there's chaos in your life.** Ask God if disobedience is feeding it. Then obey whatever He shows you.
- **Replace chaos with action.** Every time you feel anxious or stressed this week, immediately do one small act of obedience toward what God's asking. Feel worried? Text the person. Feel stressed? Take the first step. Train your body to respond to chaos with obedience, not panic.

Day 16 • The Revival Nobody Expected

At this the men greatly feared the LORD, and they offered a sacrifice to the LORD and made vows to him. Jonah 1:16 (NIV)

You won't believe what happens next. The prophet runs from God and pagan sailors end up worshiping Him. It's the revival nobody expected. These guys went from praying to random gods to fearing the Lord, offering sacrifices, and making vows. That's a full conversion. That's a revival service on a boat in the middle of the Mediterranean. And Jonah wasn't even there to see it. When we think about the revival in the Book of Jonah, we generally think of the city of Nineveh repenting. But don't miss the first revival that occurred on the ship headed to Tarshish.

So what is genuine revival? It's not hype. It's not emotional manipulation. It's not manufactured enthusiasm at a conference. Biblical revival is when God shows up in power and people encounter His reality in a way that fundamentally changes them. These sailors experienced exactly that.

Sometimes God does His best work through our worst moments. These sailors met God because of Jonah's disobedience. That doesn't make disobedience good. But it proves God's ability to bring revival out of rebellion, to create beauty from chaos, to save people even when His prophet is literally being thrown overboard.

Think about how wild that is. Jonah tried to run from preaching to Nineveh, and God used that very run to preach to sailors. God's mission can't be stopped by our disobedience. He just brings other people into the story. The gospel spreads even through our failures.

This unexpected, overlooked revival reminds us that God's reach extends beyond our obedience. He's working in places we can't see, saving people we didn't know needed saving, creating worship in the middle of our storms.

Maybe you feel like your failure has disqualified you from being used by God. Maybe you think your season of running means God's mission stalled. This verse says otherwise. God is sovereignly moving in ways you can't track. Your storm might be someone else's salvation story.

Live It Out:

- **Write down one area where God might be working** even though you can't see it yet. Trust Him with it.

- **Make one specific vow to God this week.** A concrete commitment based on what He's done in your life.

- **Post your testimony on social media.** Write one paragraph about what God has done for you. No editing for likes. Tell the truth and let revival spread.

DAY 17 · God Moves in Odd Places

The LORD appointed a great fish to swallow Jonah, and Jonah was in the belly of the fish three days and three nights.
Jonah 1:17 (CSB)

IF you had to take a guess on where the next great revival in the church is going to start, where would you say? Perhaps a college campus, a megachurch, or some kind of prayer gathering. What if I told you that one of history's greatest movements of God started in the belly of a fish?

Do you see that word *appointed?* God didn't just allow that fish to appear. He orchestrated it. He chose this fish for this prophet at this moment in time and turned it into a chamber of revival. Let that sink in for a second. Jonah was soaking wet, covered in seaweed, surrounded by stomach acid, probably having panic attacks left and right. This is the last place you'd expect God to show up and do His divine work of transformation. But that's exactly what He did.

For three days and three nights Jonah had nowhere to run, no distractions, no excuses. Just a rebellious prophet and a relentless God in the most uncomfortable of circumstances. Jonah came out three days later a changed man. Revived, recommissioned, ready to spark citywide repentance in Nineveh.

This is God's pattern throughout Scripture. Moses met God in a burning bush in the middle of nowhere. David was anointed king while feeding sheep. Paul met Jesus on a desolate road. Jesus Himself was born in a feeding trough, launched His ministry in a wilderness, recruited fishermen and tax collectors, and secured our salvation on a Roman cross.

God doesn't need perfect circumstances to bring revival. He just needs surrendered hearts. Revival doesn't wait for the perfect setting. It happens in hospital rooms and halfway houses, in prison cells and parking lots, in messy kitchens at 2 A.M., in the car after a devastating diagnosis, in the cubicle where you've been avoiding God's voice.

Stop waiting for the perfect circumstances and start surrendering your heart right where you are. God's work of revival can start today in the most unlikely place.

Live It Out

- **Surrender your circumstances.** Instead of asking God to change your situation, ask Him what He wants to teach you through it.
- **Look for God in odd places.** Pay attention this week to where and how God might be working in uncomfortable or unexpected circumstances in your life.
- **Encourage someone who's experiencing the "belly of the fish."** Reach out to someone in a difficult season and remind them that God often does His best work in our worst moments.

CHAPTER 2
The Belly and the Breakthrough

You've just spent 17 days watching Jonah run. You've seen him book the ticket to Tarshish, board the ship, sleep through the storm, get exposed, confess, and finally get thrown overboard. Chapter 1 was about the call and the run—the prophet who said no to God and paid the price. Now we enter the belly of the fish, and everything changes.

Chapter 2 isn't just about surviving; it's about surrendering. This is where Jonah stops running and starts praying. Where rebellion gives way to repentance. Where the darkest place becomes the holiest place. You're about to read one of the most honest, desperate, beautiful prayers in all of Scripture. It's important to understand the fish isn't the punishment. The fish is the rescue. God didn't send Jonah to the depths to destroy him…He sent him there to save him.

Get ready. This is where transformation begins.

DAY 18 ▪ Alone with God

Jonah prayed to the Lord his God from inside the fish.
Jonah 2:1 (CSB)

There is a moment in every crisis when you hit a wall and realize that no person is coming to rescue you. Jonah reached that moment in the belly of a fish with zero bars on his phone, no rescue team on the way, and no plan B. It was just him and the God he'd been running from, finally alone together with nowhere left to hide.

It's the first time we see Jonah pray in this entire story. He didn't pray when God first called him. He didn't pray during the storm. He didn't pray when the sailors confronted him. Only now, when every option has been exhausted and every escape route is closed, does prayer become his reality. That's when intimacy with God stops being optional and starts being survival.

Remember Day 3 when Jonah was running from God's presence? He thought he could escape. Now he's trapped in the one place where he can't avoid God. Turns out, you can run to Tarshish, but God will follow you to the bottom of the ocean. He will meet you anywhere.

Pay attention to whom he prayed. The text says *to the LORD his God (NLT)* —not a distant deity, but *his God.* The relationship was still in place even after all the running and rebellion. Your disobedience doesn't cancel God's commitment to you. Your failures don't erase His faithfulness.

Being alone with God means peeling back all the pretense we normally carry. You can't perform at the bottom. You can't fake it when drowning in consequences. We surround ourselves with people and fill our calendars to avoid being alone because being alone means facing ourselves and facing God without filters. But it's in this place that transformation happens.

Jonah could have stayed bitter, just rehearsing his grievances. But he prayed instead. That's the first step back from rebellion. Not perfection, but simply showing up in the darkness and saying, "God, I need you."

Live It Out:

- **Turn your phone grayscale for one month.** Make everything black and white. Remove the dopamine hits of color. When your phone becomes boring and you pick it up less, use that reclaimed time to pray.

- **Delete your safety nets.** Write down every person or thing you run to before you run to God. Remove access to one of them for 48 hours. When crisis hits and you can't call them, you'll have to call on God instead.

- **Cancel one thing on your calendar this week to make space for God.** Not rearrange it…cancel it. Replace it with time alone with God. Let the sacrifice create the desperation.

DAY 19 ▪ Rock Bottom Revival

He said: "I called to the LORD in my distress, and he answered me. I cried out for help from deep inside Sheol; you heard my voice."
Jonah 2:2 (CSB)

WHAT does it take for you to finally cry out to God? For some people, it's a phone call that changes everything. For others, it's a diagnosis, a betrayal, a financial collapse. For Jonah, it was three days in the belly of a fish. He called his location "Sheol," the place of the dead. Rock bottom…exactly where his revival began.

We've already seen one revival in this book. Pagan sailors on a storm-tossed ship encountered the living God and were transformed. Now we're seeing a second revival unfold in the darkest, most unlikely place imaginable: inside a fish, where a rebellious prophet finally stops running and starts praying.

What's your rock bottom? Have you hit it yet or are you still trying to avoid it?

This is Jonah's testimony. *"I called to the LORD in my distress" (CSB).* Not in his comfort. Not in his success. In his distress. When everything fell apart. When he had nowhere else to turn. In that moment, he called. And God didn't ignore him. God answered. Immediately. Completely. Revival often begins with a cry from the depths when you have no other options.

Sometimes you have to hit bottom before you look up. Sometimes you have to exhaust every alternative before you turn to the only One who can actually save you. This isn't God being cruel. That's you finally getting honest enough to stop pretending you can handle it. To cry out from the depths and mean it.

What would it take for you to get that honest? Or are you already there and just haven't admitted it yet?

The revival didn't come when things got better. It came at the lowest point. When Jonah stopped running and started praying. When he stopped blaming and started crying out. When he traded his pride for humility. That's where God meets you. Not when you've cleaned yourself up. Not when you've got it all figured out. But when you're crying out from Sheol, "God I need you and I can't do this alone." That's when revival breaks out.

Live It Out:

- **Pray Jonah's prayer from your low place.** Kneel where you are most distressed and read Jonah 2:2 aloud: *"I called to the LORD in my distress, and he answered me."* Don't get up until you mean it.

- **Don't pray hypocrisy.** Set a timer for 5 minutes. Pray with ruthless honesty about where you are, not where you want to be. No churchy words. No act. Only the raw truth from the pit.
- **Read Psalm 130 out loud** every morning this week before anything else. While still in bed. Before coffee or phone. Let ancient rock-bottom prayers teach you how to pray from your depths.

DAY 20 ▪ Below the Surface

"You hurled me into the depths, into the very heart of the seas, and the currents swirled about me; all your waves and breakers swept over me." Jonah 2:3 (NIV)

SOME lessons can only be learned underwater. Below the surface. Under pressure. In the dark. In the silence. Jonah did not encounter God in a temple or on a mountaintop. He found Him in the undertow, in a place no one else could see. This is where faith stops performing and starts surviving.

We miss that God always does His best work when no one is watching, when you are invisible to everyone else. The deepest change never happens on stages or in spotlight moments. It takes place in the dark, in the deep, where only you and God are present.

Jonah hit rock bottom…literally to the foundation of the mountains. The gates of death shut behind him. This was as deep as it gets. The very lowest point. And this is where God found him.

Think of Christ. Three days in a tomb. Hidden. Dead to the world. Yet this is where resurrection power began to stir. Below the surface is where death became life, where the greatest victory in history happened in utter darkness.

How deep have you gone? Do you believe God can reach you there? Maybe you're drowning in shame from last weekend. Or isolation so thick you haven't answered a text in days. Or an addiction you can't shake. Have you told yourself so many times you're too far gone, too broken, too much of a mess that you no longer believe He's coming for you?

God is the lifter of the lowly, the rescuer of the drowned. The same God who lifted Jonah up from the sea floor lifted Christ from the tomb. And He can lift you up from whatever is pulling you under right now. The depths are not the end. They are where God always does His deepest work.

Live It Out:

- **Rewrite Jonah 2:3 in your own words** based on your life right now. Substitute "depths" and "seas" with whatever is drowning you. Make it personal.

- **Read the resurrection account in Matthew 28** every day this week. Meditate on what happened below the surface in that tomb. Let Christ's hidden victory give you hope for your hidden struggle.

- **Start a private note** on your phone called "Below the Surface." Each day this week, jot one sentence about what God is doing in you that no one else can see. Observe how the invisible work begins to bubble up to the surface over time.

DAY 21 ▪ Ghosted by God

"But I said, 'I have been banished from your sight, yet I will look once more toward your holy temple.'"   *Jonah 2:4 (CSB)*

JONAH is underwater, alone, and convinced God is done with him. *"I have been banished from your sight"* (CSB). Not "I feel distant" or "I'm struggling to connect." Banished. Exiled. Cut off. Like God saw him, said, "We're done here," and walked away.

This is different than just feeling like your prayers aren't working. This is the suffocating certainty that you've crossed a line you can't uncross. That you ran too far, sinned too much, disappointed God one too many times. And now there's radio silence. Not because God's testing you or teaching you patience, but because He's actually gone.

That's the lie Jonah believed in the fish belly. Separated from everything. Drowning in consequences. No light. No air. No escape. The worst part wasn't the physical isolation but the spiritual one. The bone-deep terror that he'd finally done it and finally pushed God away for good.

Maybe that's where you are. Not in a fish, but in the aftermath of the affair, the relapse, the abortion, the betrayal, the thing you swore you'd never do and did anyway. And now you can't shake the feeling that God's looking at you differently. That the door closed. That you're on the outside now and there's no getting back in.

"Yet I will look once more toward your holy temple" (CSB). That word, *yet,* changes everything. Everything before it says you're finished. Everything after it says you're not. Jonah couldn't see God, couldn't feel Him. He had zero

evidence God was still there, yet he said, "I'm going to look one more time."

Not because he felt hopeful but because he decided to. Not because the feelings came first but because the choice came first. One more glance toward where God lives even when every nerve in your body screams He's not looking back.

Here's what Jonah didn't know yet. God never left. The banishment was in Jonah's head, not in God's heart. The distance was real, but it wasn't permanent. And the *once more* he was forcing himself to do was the exact moment God was already moving to pull him out.

The silence doesn't mean absence. Sometimes God is quietest when He's closest, working in ways you can't see, moving in the dark where you can't track Him, preparing the rescue while you're convinced you're abandoned.

One more time. That's all it takes. One more prayer into the void. One more glance toward the temple when you're sure no one's home. One more choice to look up when everything in you wants to give up.

Live It Out:

- **Pray when you're not feeling it.** If you're feeling like God has ghosted you right now, look toward Him anyway.

- **Remember when God first showed up for you** in your life. Write it down. Keep a record of that so you don't forget that God can be seen and felt.

- **Give God some praise**. Spend a few minutes thanking God for not abandoning you.

DAY 22 ▪ Die Daily

"The water engulfed me up to the neck; the watery depths overcame me; seaweed was wrapped around my head. I sank to the foundations of the mountains, the earth's gates shut behind me forever!" Jonah 2:5-6 (CSB)

JONAH didn't just hit rock bottom in that fish. He hit the grave. The earth's gates shut behind him forever. God was putting the old prophet to death so a new one could emerge. The thing is, what happened to Jonah once needs to happen to you daily. Die to the version of yourself that runs. Die to the version that rebels. Die to the version that thinks it can control the outcome.

When he came up out of the fish, what happened next wasn't physical death but it was close enough. The earth's gates shut behind him. That is tomb language. That is burial imagery. Jonah went down into the depths, felt the weight of death, and came back up. Sound familiar? It should. It's a preview of what Jesus would do centuries later and what every Christian experiences spiritually.

This forced death in the fish ripped away everything Jonah thought he had control over. The earth's gates shutting behind him was significant. Final. Complete. There was no going back. The old Jonah that ran needed to die. The old Jonah that rebelled needed to die. The old Jonah that thought he could outrun God needed to die. The new Jonah who would obey, who would preach, who would represent God could only come after the old one was buried.

What needs to die in you today? What version of yourself are you trying to hold on to that God is asking you to bury? Maybe it's the version that needs everyone's approval. Maybe it's the version of you that's controlled by fear, or maybe it's holding a grudge. "Die daily" means you let that go. You let the gates shut on it, you stop trying to resurrect what God has already crucified.

Live It Out:

- **Give away one of your favorite possessions.** Not donate. Actually give it to someone by name. The thing you love most. Hand it to them this week and say, "This represented who I used to be. I'm letting it die." Let the loss be real and permanent.
- **Go anonymous.** Pick something you're genuinely good at, something you normally get recognized for. Do it completely anonymously for one week. No credit. No acknowledgment. Let your need for recognition die. If no one knows you did it, does it still matter?
- **Read Romans 6:1-14.** Let Paul's words about dying to sin and living to God reshape how you see your daily walk.

DAY 23 ▪ You Raised My Life

"The water engulfed me up to the neck; the watery depths overcame me; seaweed was wrapped around my head. I sank to the foundations of the mountains, the earth's gates shut behind me forever! Then you raised my life from the Pit, LORD my God!" Jonah 2:5-6 (CSB)

DROWNING people don't look like they're drowning. They're often silent, barely moving, slipping under while everyone around them thinks they're fine. God sees past the performance. He sees the seaweed wrapped around your head. He sees the water at your neck. He sees you slipping under when no one else notices. And He doesn't wait for you to make it back to the surface on your own. He reaches down and lifts.

Have you ever been caught in an undertow at the beach? It's terrifying. The ocean pulls you under, drags you out and no amount of swimming helps. Lifeguards will tell you not to fight it. You can't win against the current. Your only hope is someone on shore who sees you struggling and comes in after you.

Jonah was past the undertow. He'd stopped struggling. Water over his neck. Sinking to depths where even light doesn't reach. And then God dove in. Not because Jonah called the loudest or swam the hardest, but because that's what God does. He rescues people from currents they can't escape and depths they can't survive.

This is the turnaround moment. Water up to his neck. Sinking to the foundations of the mountains. The gates of death closing behind him forever. *Then…* That one word changed his whole direction. *Then you raised my life (CSB).*

Jonah sank to the foundations of the mountains. That's as deep as it gets. The absolute bottom of everything. Even there, God reached down and pulled him up. There's no pit too deep for God's reach. You might feel like you're at the foundations right now. Like the earth's gates have shut behind you. Like there's no way back. But God specializes in lifting lives from places where everyone else has given up.

What foundation have you sunk to? And do you actually believe God can reach you there, or have you convinced yourself you're too far gone?

You raised my life (CSB) is past tense for Jonah because he's telling the story after the rescue. But it can be future tense for you. If you're still sinking, still tangled, still at the bottom, know that God can lift you. He's done it before. He'll do it again. The same God who raised Jonah from the Pit can raise you from yours. Celebrate that. Let the wonder of it hit you. God lifts lives.

Live It Out:

- **Name what has you tangled up.** The addiction, the relationship, the fear, the secret. Ask God specifically to untangle you and cut you free from what's pulling you under.

- **Stop pretending you can save yourself.** Write these words on paper: "I'm drowning and I can't save myself. Jesus, lift my life." Then text a Christian friend or pastor and tell them you just surrendered your life to Christ. Let today be your rescue day.

- **Thank God for a time He lifted you from a pit.** If you're in one now, thank Him in advance for the rescue that's coming. Believe it's already done.

Day 24 ▪ On 1% Battery

"As my life was slipping away, I remembered the LORD. And my earnest prayer went out to you in your holy Temple."
Jonah 2:7 (NLT)

ON 1% battery. That's where Jonah was. *Life slipping away (NLT).* Everything shutting down. In that moment, with nothing left, he remembered the Lord. Not when things were good. Not when he was strong. But when he was dying and about to power off completely.

As my life was slipping away (NLT) is not just exhaustion language. It's death language. Jonah was dying in that fish, and he knew it. The oxygen was running out. The strength was gone. The hope was dimming. And at that moment of death, he *remembered the Lord (NLT)*. His prayer went up to God's holy temple.

This is what it means to be crucified with Christ. Paul says it in Galatians 2:20: *I have been crucified with Christ, and I no longer live, but Christ lives in me (CSB)*. Real Christianity is not a process of life management. It's not a path to self-help or self-actualization. It's not about learning how to balance your life. It's about dying. Your old self, your old way, your old control, all of it has to fade away. And when it does, when you're down to nothing, that's when Christ becomes everything.

Jonah's life was slipping, but his prayer was rising. That's the gospel paradox. You have to go down before you go up. You have to die before you live. You have to lose everything before you gain Christ. The old you doesn't get a software update. It gets crucified.

So what happens when your life is slipping away? When your plans collapse? When your strength runs out? When your control disappears? That's the moment you discover what you're really living for. If you've built your life on Christ, He's what you remember. If you've died with Him, you'll rise with Him. But if you've been living for yourself, trying to maintain your own kingdom, when crisis hits you'll have nothing left but panic.

On 1% battery is a crucifixion moment. It's where the old you dies and Christ becomes your only hope. Jonah remembered the Lord because in that moment of death, God was all he had left. And God was enough.

Live It Out:

- **Play the highlight reel.** Write down three specific memories of times God showed up for you. Keep this list where you can see it when you're running low.
- **Pray from the bottom.** If you're at 1% battery right now, remember the Lord. Pray even if it's just one sentence. Your prayer will reach Him.
- **Build your spiritual reserves.** Spend time with God when you don't need anything so that when you do, you'll have history to draw from.

DAY 25 ▪ My Idols Are Making Me Idle

"Those who cling to worthless idols turn away from God's love for them." Jonah 2:8 (NIV)

A TREADMILL is great for exercise but terrible for travel. You can run for hours and never leave the room. What happens when you worship idols? You're working. You're moving. You're exhausted. But you're not going anywhere. You're just burning energy on something that was never designed to take you where you need to go. Your idols are making you idle.

This verse hits different. Jonah just dropped a truth bomb from the belly of a fish. When you worship worthless things, you abandon your own mercy. Idolatry doesn't just offend God; it costs you the very thing you need most, the mercy that could save you.

Consider what's been keeping you idle lately. What's draining your energy without giving anything back? What are you chasing that's making you stagnant in your relationship with God? What are you holding onto that's keeping you from receiving the mercy He's extending? That's your idol. It's time to name it.

Jonah figured this out in the fish. Surrounded by darkness. Out of options. Facing death. He realized the things he'd been chasing were worthless. They couldn't save him. They couldn't satisfy him. They couldn't do what only God could do. So he let them go. He turned from the idols and turned toward mercy. He moved. This is how you go from idle to active in your faith again.

Live It Out:
- **Track your treadmill.** Set a timer every time you engage with your idol this week (scroll social media, check your ex's profile, online shop, binge shows). At week's end, total the hours. Then ask, "If I'd spent this time pursuing God instead, where would I be right now?"
- **Build an anti-shrine.** Take the space where you worship your idol (phone home screen, favorite chair, specific website) and fill it with Scripture instead. New wallpaper with Jonah 2:8. Sticky notes with truth. Make worshiping your idol require going through God's Word first.
- **Write a eulogy.** Write a goodbye letter to your idol. "Dear [TikTok/relationship/achievement], you promised me _____ but only gave me _____. I'm letting you go because God's mercy is better." Read it out loud, then delete or destroy it.

DAY 26 ▪ Eyes Wide Open

"But as for me, I will sacrifice to you with a voice of thanksgiving. I will fulfill what I have vowed. Salvation belongs to the LORD!"
Jonah 2:9 (CSB)

JONAH was buried alive, famished, and choking in a fish's belly with seaweed and stomach acid all around him. But his eyes were wide open to see what mattered most: *"Salvation belongs to the LORD"* *(CSB)*. This is not Jonah's private revelation; this is the theological undercurrent of every revival the world has ever seen. Muddy it up and revival becomes a project, a program, and something predictable. Clarify it and revival becomes what it has always been, God's sovereign work through surrendered people.

We often get stuck here. We long for revival but we want to control it. We long for God to move but on our timeline, through our methods, and proving the merit of our efforts. We pray for awakening while secretly suspecting if we could just get the formula right (the right worship, the right preaching, the right programs, the right strategy) we could manufacture what only God can do.

Jonah shows us the opposite. Jonah couldn't make the sailors worship, quiet the storm, survive the sea, nor digest himself out of the fish. Every human effort failed. As a result of that failure, Jonah's eyes were wide open. He finally saw what he'd been blind to all along: salvation comes only from the Lord.

After Jonah declared, *"Salvation belongs to the Lord"* *(CSB)*, God spoke to the fish, the fish vomited Jonah onto dry land, and suddenly Jonah was on his way to Nineveh. The revival that took place in Nineveh did not happen because Jonah finally got his act together. It happened because Jonah finally surrendered to the God who owns salvation.

This declaration frees us. We are not responsible for producing revival; we are responsible for surrendering to the God who does. We are not the source; we are the vessel. When God uses surrendered vessels the world knows who deserves the glory.

Stop trying to manufacture revival and start surrendering to the God who owns it. Open your eyes to see that salvation belongs to Him alone.

Live It Out:

- **Conversationally share how God rescued you.** This week, tell someone you care about the power statement, "Salvation belongs to the Lord."
- **Surrender Control:** Identify one area where you've been trying to control spiritual outcomes and consciously surrender it to God's sovereignty.
- **Position Yourself:** Instead of trying to instigate revival, focus on positioning yourself as a surrendered vessel through prayer, worship, and obedience.

DAY 27 ▪ Launched

And the LORD commanded the fish, and it vomited Jonah onto dry land.   Jonah 2:10 (BSB)

THE same moment Jonah was expelled from the fish was the moment he was propelled into his calling. Launched. Not gently released. Not carefully delivered. Violently ejected onto a beach in the most humiliating way possible. That disgusting exit became his entrance into the greatest revival mission in the Old Testament.

Sometimes your rescue looks worse than your crisis. Sometimes freedom feels like failure. Sometimes God's deliverance doesn't come with dignity attached. But we miss that the mess is often the momentum. What expelled you might be exactly what propels you forward.

Jonah's been crying out for rescue for three days. And God answers. But the answer is getting puked onto a beach covered in fish guts and seaweed. That's the launch? Yes. That's the launch. The most humiliating exit imaginable becomes the most powerful entrance into purpose.

Notice who's in control here. *The LORD commanded the fish (NIV).* Not the fish deciding on its own. Not Jonah negotiating his way out. God commanded and the fish obeyed. Remember Day 17 when the fish swallowed Jonah? That was God's appointment. This is God's command. Both moments are rescue. The fish saved Jonah from drowning. Now the fish launches Jonah into obedience.

God's launch strategy values your life more than your reputation. He cares more about your mission than your image. Jonah was alive. He was on dry land. He was within walking distance of Nineveh. And from that gross, humiliating moment, Jonah got launched into the assignment he'd been running from.

Your launch will probably not be glamorous, but it will be effective. God doesn't need your aesthetic approval. He just needs your willingness to be launched.

Live It Out:

- **Make a list of three things** you lost recently. Next to each one, write what space or capacity that loss created. Ask God to show you what He's preparing to launch into that new space.
- **Identify what expelled you recently.** Job loss. Breakup. Failure. Now ask, "Could this be God launching me into something new?" Journal about where this might be propelling you.
- **Take a photo of yourself right now, post-mess, post-crisis, post-whatever just happened.** Save it as "Launch Day." This isn't rock bottom. This is your launch pad. God's about to propel you forward.

CHAPTER 3
The Message and the Mercy

THE fish spits him out onto dry land, and now Jonah is standing on the beach literally covered in seaweed and stomach acid. I can only imagine he reeks of death itself. But what's next? Is he going to run again? Will he make excuses? Will he negotiate with God how his calling will go?

Chapter 3 deals with second chances and what happens when a hesitant prophet finally does what he's told. Jonah goes to Nineveh, declares the message, and God shows up in the most unforeseen way imaginable… The whole city repents! All 120,000 people. The king himself gets off his throne, puts on sackcloth, and calls for a citywide fast. But Jonah's heart hasn't fully changed.

It's the greatest revival in the Old Testament. And it's about to make Jonah furious. Sometimes obedience exposes what grace hasn't yet healed in us. Let's see what happens when mercy wins.

DAY 28 ▪ Not Finished Yet

Then the word of the LORD came to Jonah a second time.
Jonah 3:1 (BSB)

IF you've ever played sports, you know what it's like to get benched. You messed up. Coach yanked you out of the game. You're sitting there on the sidelines sulking, watching everyone else have fun. You start to wonder, "Will I ever get to play again?" Then, out of nowhere, the coach looks right at you and says, "Get ready. You're going back in."

That's Jonah. God benched him for running away. But God didn't bench Jonah for good. *The word of the* LORD *came to Jonah a second time (NIV)*. He was going back into the game.

The word of the LORD *came to Jonah (NIV)*. Again. Just like Day 1. Same call. Same prophet. Different heart. God didn't change His mind about Nineveh, and He didn't change His mind about Jonah. Remember, God's calling on your life doesn't expire just because you failed the first time.

God doesn't give up easily. That's the message of this verse. Jonah ran. Got thrown into the sea. Spent three days in the belly of a fish. Got vomited up onto a beach. You'd think that would be the end of the story. But no. *The word of the* LORD *came to Jonah a second time (BSB)*. God wasn't finished with Jonah. His calling hadn't been canceled. The mission was still on.

Maybe you've been sitting on the bench this year wondering if God is finished with you. Wondering if you messed up so badly He won't give you another chance. Wondering if your purpose died in the fish. This verse is for you. God is not finished yet. He's still speaking. Still calling. Still offering you a chance to live out what He created you for.

The word of the LORD *came to Jonah a second time (BSB)* means God isn't holding grudges. He's not keeping track of your wrongs to disqualify you later. He's moving forward. And He's inviting you to move forward with Him. What you do with that second chance is up to you. But the chance is there. The door is open. God is speaking. Again.

Live It Out:

- **Stop for a moment** and thank God for all the times God didn't give up on you.

- **Encourage someone** who feels their bad choices have disqualified them. Use your words to reignite their faith.

- **Reject the lie.** If you've been thinking God is done with you because of past failures, stop today. He's not finished yet. Believe it. Act on it.

Day 29 ▪ Get Back in the Game

"Get up and go to the great city of Nineveh, and deliver the message I have given you." Jonah 3:2 (NLT)

I HAVE teenagers. This means that sometimes the trash is full, the yard is not cut, there is random food left all around the house. My kids kind of listen when I tell them, "Clean your room," or "Do your chores." But truthfully, sometimes what I say seemingly falls on deaf ears. Then I have to say it again.

How many times has God had to repeat Himself to you? What does it say about us that we need to hear the same thing twice or ten times before we actually move?

When your boss, parent, or friend says something again it tends to have more urgency. It's more serious. The first time might be a request. The second time is a test of whether or not you were actually listening. That's exactly what's happening here with Jonah. God tells him to *get up and go to Nineveh (NLT)* for the second time.

But notice what God doesn't say. He doesn't rehash the fish incident. He doesn't make Jonah apologize a thousand times. He doesn't put him on spiritual probation or make him prove himself first. God just repeats the original call. Same city. Same mission. Same urgency. The calling doesn't change just because you failed the first time. Your assignment is still waiting.

So what's your Nineveh? What's the thing God keeps bringing up that you keep avoiding? And how long are you planning to make Him wait?

Stop sitting in your failure. Stop camping in your past mistakes. Stop letting what happened to you become an excuse for not doing what God is asking you to do now. The command hasn't changed. The calling is still there. And God is saying, "Get up."

You've been in the fish long enough. You've replayed the failure enough times. You've punished yourself sufficiently. God isn't asking you to forget what happened. He's asking you to get up anyway.

Second chances come with the same expectations as first chances. God's grace gives you another opportunity, but it doesn't lower the bar. He still wants your obedience, your faithfulness, your willingness to go where He sends you and say what He tells you to say.

Live It Out:

- **Do a physical "get up" challenge.** Every time you think about your calling this week, drop and do 10 push-ups or jump up-and-down 10 times. Train your body to associate God's call with immediate action, not hesitation.

- **Create a message deadline.** Ask God what He wants you to say. Write it on a sticky note with today's date. Put it on your dashboard or bathroom mirror. You have 7 days to deliver it. Let the countdown push you past comfortable.

- **The Voice-Memo Challenge:** Record a 60-second voice memo on your phone right now. Say your name, today's date, and what you're committing to do to get back in the game. Be specific. Save it. Play it back every morning this week before you check anything else on your phone. Let your own voice call you back to obedience.

DAY 30 ▪ Better Late than Never

Jonah got up and went to Nineveh, just as the LORD had commanded. (Nineveh was a very large city, three days' journey.) Jonah 3:3 (CSB)

MOST of us don't get do-overs. Miss a job interview, and they find another worker. Sleep through the opportunity, and it goes to someone else. Run from your calling, and that's usually it. But Jonah ran from God and God gave him another chance at the same mission. Just one fish-shaped detour later. That's grace when God's purposes are bigger than your failures.

Imagine walking into Nineveh after everyone knows you ran. The sailors have been telling your story in every port. "Yeah, that's the prophet who tried to run from God. Got swallowed by a fish. Showed up three months late covered in fish guts." Late obedience means showing up with a story and a past. But it's still better than not showing up at all.

Your friends bought houses; you're living with roommates. They're married with kids; you're still figuring out who you are. They found their calling in college; you're just now starting. Late feels like failure.

But late is still in the game. Your timeline doesn't disqualify you from your purpose.

Maybe you think you missed the window, missed the season, missed your shot. But if God is still bringing it up, it's not too late. If the calling is still bothering you, the door is still open. Jonah learned this in the worst way possible. God's assignments don't come with expiration dates.

Finally, Jonah got up. He went. He obeyed. Not immediately like he should have back in Chapter 1. Not without a detour through rebellion and a fish. But he did it. And that's what matters. He didn't let his past failure keep him from future obedience.

Being late costs you time, energy, opportunities, and peace. Jonah lost all of that. But what he didn't lose was his calling. What he didn't lose was God's willingness to use him. What he didn't lose was the chance to fulfill his purpose.

Late is better than never. Not because late is ideal. Not because delay doesn't matter. But because God's purposes are bigger than your timeline. Your calling doesn't expire. Your assignment is still waiting. And God is still saying, "It's not too late. Just go."

Live It Out:

- **Book your Nineveh ticket.** Buy the plane ticket, register for the class, or schedule the appointment you've been delaying. Make it real with money and a date. Let financial commitment force you to finally show up.

- **Resurrection Sunday restart.** Jesus' resurrection proves it's never too late for new life. Pick a day and declare it your personal resurrection day. Let the dead thing in you come back to life through obedience.

- **Write your "finally" prayer.** Jonah finally got up and went. Write a prayer that starts with "Lord, I'm finally ready to..." Then do the thing you just prayed about within 48 hours.

Day 31 ▪ Serving Notice

On the day Jonah entered the city, he shouted to the crowds: "Forty days from now Nineveh will be destroyed!" Jonah 3:4 (NLT)

SOME words kill your career before you finish the sentence. Whistleblowing on your own company. Calling out corruption in a room full of power players. Telling a tyrant he's wrong to his face. These are the speeches that end jobs, wreck reputations, and sometimes get you killed.

Jonah gave that speech. He walked into Nineveh (the most violent, oppressive empire on earth) and announced their destruction. This wasn't a TED Talk. This wasn't carefully crafted to get applause. He marched straight into enemy territory with a message no one wanted to hear. No introduction. No warm-up. No building rapport first. Just straight to the point: *"Forty days from now Nineveh will be destroyed!"* (NLT)

That's bold. That's uncomfortable. That's obedience. Jonah wasn't there to negotiate or sugarcoat. God expected His messenger to deliver His word without alteration because it needed to be precise, immediate, and absolute.

Notice that God gave warning. Forty days. Not "tomorrow you're done." Not "you're already finished."

Forty days. That's a grace period. Even in judgment, there's mercy. Even in the warning, there's hope. Even in giving notice, God's providing them time to respond. God's not just pronouncing doom. He's inviting change. The notice includes the deadline and the opportunity. Both matter.

Jonah has no idea what's about to happen. He thinks he's pronouncing doom. He has no clue he's about to witness the most dramatic mass repentance in history. Sometimes our obedience sets up miracles we never expected. Sometimes the hard message we deliver becomes the catalyst for revival we couldn't imagine. God uses our willingness even when we can't see what He's doing.

Bold obedience looks different in your life. It's speaking truth even when it's uncomfortable. It's delivering the message God gives you even when you know it won't be popular. Maybe God has been prompting you to have a hard conversation with someone. Maybe He's asking you to speak up about something at work or in your community. Maybe He's calling you to share your faith with someone who doesn't want to hear it.

Ask yourself, "Is it God's message or your frustration?" Jonah delivered what God told him, not what he felt. Make sure you're speaking God's truth, not just your truth. The temptation is to soften the message or to weaponize it. But sometimes God just wants you to deliver the notice. Plain. Clear. Direct. "This is what God says." Then trust Him with the results. Your job is obedience, not outcome.

Live It Out:

- **Speak truth with love and courage.** The same God who warned Nineveh now welcomes sinners through His Son. This week, be a messenger of mercy. Find someone far from God and challenge them to turn from their sins.

- **Watch the watchman.** Every morning this week, read Ezekiel 33:1-9 about the prophets' call to watch and warn. Let God's word about speaking warnings convict you.

- **Screenshot this devotional.** Send it to the person who needs to hear truth from you with this message: "I read this today. We need to talk this week." Let the devotional open the door. Then walk through it.

DAY 32 ▪ Revival Is for Everybody

Then the people of Nineveh believed God. They proclaimed a fast and dressed in sackcloth—from the greatest of them to the least.
Jonah 3:5 (CSB)

ONE day Jonah is preaching to a hard city. The next day revival breaks out in the streets and sweeps through the city like wildfire. The people of Nineveh believed God. They didn't just believe Jonah; they believed God. Revival breaks out when people suddenly realize that God is real; when they get a fresh view of His goodness and holiness, His mercy and His majesty.

The entire city was stirred up. Elites were humbled, commoners were crying out to God, pride vanished, pretenses were dropped, conviction spread faster than rumor. That's what real revival does. It breaks down social barriers and levels the playing field.

This wasn't just an Old Testament miracle. It has happened in the 21st century as well. One of the greatest revivals of the last century was the 1970 Asbury Revival in Kentucky. It didn't start with a conference or a church-wide outreach campaign. It started in the middle of a normal college worship service. When a few students responded to the presence of God with repentance and confession, suddenly more and more people joined them. Within hours the chapel was packed, within days the whole town was packed, and people came from across the country just to experience what God was doing. Revival doesn't need a platform; it just needs people who are surrendered.

Nineveh's story should remind us that revival doesn't need a perfect backdrop; it just needs responsive hearts. It doesn't need to start with the most influential people; it comes through people who are willing. It begins when God sovereignly chooses a place, often where we least expect it.

Jonah's preaching was subpar, but their response was miraculous. They took God seriously with no delay, no negotiation, no "let me think about it." Revival caught momentum because obedience was swift. Can you imagine what God could do in your neighborhood if people responded like that? Or in your home if your family would respond like that? Revival might not start on a stage; it might start in a living room or in a conversation at the local coffee shop.

Stop waiting for revival to start somewhere else and start being the kind of person who responds immediately to God's voice. Revival can break out anywhere that people open their hearts to what God wants to do.

Live It Out:

- **Respond immediately.** The next time you sense God leading you to do something, obey without delay or negotiation.
- **Pray for your community.** Spend time this week praying specifically for spiritual awakening to break out in your neighborhood, workplace, or social circle.
- **Be available.** Like Jonah, look for opportunities to share God's message of salvation with people from different backgrounds.

DAY 33 ▪ Villains and the Good News

When word reached the king of Nineveh, he got up from his throne, took off his royal robe, put on sackcloth, and sat in ashes.
Jonah 3:6 (CSB)

IMAGINE the worst villain you've ever seen on the big screen. Picture Sauron, that dark lord, using his army of orcs to terrorize Middle Earth. Or picture Palpatine, that evil emperor who, as he gains control of the galaxy, rules through fear. These kinds of villains scare us because they're pure evil. We're pumped up and ready to take them down at the movies. We never expect for them to repent, to pray to God. But what if one of them took off his dark robe and fell on his knees weeping before God? "No way!" we'd say. "Impossible."

But that's exactly what happened in the Assyrian Empire. This is the king of Nineveh. He was a real-life villain, a bad guy who went around the ancient world with a reputation for murder and tyranny. Assyrians were the Nazis of their day, known for being brutally evil and leaving mountains of skulls in their wake. This is the villain Jonah was sent to confront. This was the Nineveh equivalent of a real life Palpatine, an actual flesh and blood Sauron. This king was evil incarnate, then God's word struck him.

He got up from his throne, took off his royal robe, put on sackcloth, and sat in ashes (CSB). The most powerful, vile character was completely undone. This is what revival looks like. God's word penetrates the most unlikely place and transforms the most impossible person. The king never had to be visited by the prophet. Word just reached him. A proclamation went out from a foreign preacher, telling people about a foreign God. Something crashed into the palace that human strategy can't manufacture: real, genuine conviction.

He got up, he took off, he put on, he sat down. The most powerful man in the empire does the most humble thing in response to God. When heaven invades earth, thrones empty, pride crumbles, control surrenders.

This wasn't strategy. This was not technique. This was the living God moving, orchestrating power through the most unlikely vessel. Jonah was a failed runaway prophet, literally fresh from three days in the belly of a fish. God does not need the perfect set of circumstances to move. He moves through restored failures to birth awakening in the most impossible of places.

Start believing God's grace is for everyone. Your willingness to share the gospel with "bad" people is the ultimate testament to your grasp of how good God's grace really is.

Live It Out:

- **Pray for villains.** Identify your Sauron (personally or publicly) and pray specifically for their salvation this week.

- **Examine your prejudice.** Ask God to reveal any groups of people you've written off as "too bad" for the gospel and repent of limiting His grace.

- **Share with the "unreachable."** Look for an opportunity to share the gospel with someone others might consider beyond hope, trusting that God's grace is bigger than their sin.

DAY 34 ▪ Your Feelings Don't Really Matter

Then the king and his nobles sent this decree throughout the city: "No one, not even the animals from your herds and flocks, may eat or drink anything at all. People and animals alike must wear garments of mourning, and everyone must pray earnestly to God. They must turn from their evil ways and stop all their violence." Jonah 3:7–8 (NLT)

YOUR feelings don't really matter when it comes to obedience. The king of Nineveh didn't feel like humbling himself. The people didn't feel like giving up their sinful lifestyles. Nobody felt like fasting or wearing uncomfortable sackcloth. But they did it anyway because they understood that feelings follow obedience, not the other way around. Real awakening doesn't begin with feelings; it starts with people who are willing to change.

The king didn't just feel bad about sin. He didn't schedule a prayer meeting to discuss their spiritual condition. He issued a decree that demanded transformation. Everyone had to *turn from their evil ways (NLT)* immediately. Not tomorrow, not after processing, not after giving it some thought. Now. This is what happens when God's movement becomes personal conviction and public transformation.

These weren't nice people having a spiritual awakening. Nineveh was the capital of Assyria, Israel's most brutal enemies. These were people who tortured captives, destroyed cities, terrorized the ancient world. The worst people imaginable, yet God sparked revival in them through the least likely messenger.

Here's the irony: God used a failed, bitter prophet who didn't even want the people to repent. Jonah gave the most half-hearted sermon in the Bible, eight words in Hebrew. No altar call. No follow-up strategy. He was literally hoping they would reject God's message. Yet his reluctant, angry preaching sparked the greatest revival in the Old Testament.

The word "turn" means to pivot 180 degrees and go the other way. That's what genuine awakening produces: not a better version of your old life, but total redirection. God watches what we do, not just what we say. We can cry during worship and still walk in darkness. We can feel moved by a sermon and never actually move at all.

Stop letting your feelings dictate your obedience and start letting your obedience shape your feelings. Choose to do what God says is right, even when you don't feel like it, trusting that your emotions will eventually align with your actions.

Live It Out:

- **Obey despite feelings.** Identify one area where you've been waiting to "feel like" obeying God and choose to act in obedience this week regardless of your emotions.

- **Challenge emotional decisions.** Examine one recent decision you made based primarily on feelings and ask whether it aligned with God's word and His will for your life.
- **Practice discipline.** Choose one spiritual discipline (prayer, Bible reading, service) and commit to it daily this week, even on days when you don't feel motivated.

Day 35 ▪ Who Knows?

"Who knows? God may turn and relent; he may turn from his burning anger so that we will not perish."   Jonah 3:9 (CSB)

We all have that family member. The one who we are certain will never change. We've all got that city or circumstance or person we've written off. But what if you're wrong? The king of Nineveh looked at his lost city and said two words that changed everything, *"Who knows?" (CSB)* Not "probably not," not "it's too late." Just "Who knows?" Two words that released the most improbable revival in history.

Nineveh was the worst of the worst. Violent. Wicked. Forty days from complete destruction. Everyone, including Jonah, believed they deserved to be judged. But the king refused to say it was over. He led radical repentance and proclaimed, "Who knows what God might do?" Not denial. Hope that God is greater than our worst. Hope that mercy can arrive when judgment seems sure. Hope that transformation is possible even when it seems impossible.

The king's "who knows?" echoes through Scripture. Think about Esther approaching the king uninvited, risking her life for her people. She could have said, "He'll never listen." Instead, her uncle, Mordecai, challenged her with the possibility that she'd come to the kingdom "for such a time as this." Who knows what God might do through one brave act?

Or consider the four lepers outside Samaria's gates during a famine. They were starving, the city was starving, enemies surrounded them. They said to each other, "Why should we sit here until we die? If we go into the city, we'll die. If we stay here, we'll die. So let's go to the enemy camp. If they spare us, we live. If they kill us, we die anyway." Who knows? That choice led to discovering the enemy had fled, and an entire city was saved from starvation.

The king didn't know if God would relent. He just refused to give up without trying. His refusal changed 120,000 lives. Never write people off. Never. The prodigal who refuses to come home? Who knows? The coworker hostile to faith? Who knows? The city that seems spiritually dead? Who knows what God might do if we won't give up?

We love guarantees. We want to know what God will do before we invest. We want proof of how He will respond before we act. But revival doesn't work like that. Revival comes when somebody says, "Who knows?" and acts anyway. The king taught us you don't need certainty. You need hope. You don't need to know they will change. You need to believe God can change them.

Who knows what God might do with that one conversation, that one invitation, that one prayer you stopped praying because it seemed pointless? Stop writing people off. Start hoping in God's power to do the impossible. Refuse to give up on the seemingly hopeless, trusting that God's grace is greater than any mess.

Live It Out:

- **Pray "who knows?" prayers.** Identify your most impossible situation and spend time praying, "Who knows what God might do?" instead of trying to figure out solutions yourself.
- **Study His character.** Choose one attribute of God's character (mercy, grace, love, power) and let it fuel your hope in an impossible situation this week.
- **Refuse to quit.** Think of someone you've given up on and commit to praying for them again, asking God to do what only He can do in their life.

DAY 36 ▪ Mercy Ruled

When God saw what they did and how they turned from their evil ways, he relented and did not bring on them the destruction he had threatened.   Jonah 3:10 (NIV)

I RECENTLY attended a high school football game that was "mercy ruled." The home team was up 46-0 at halftime, so the refs called the game. Can you imagine losing 92-0? The mercy rule exists to stop unnecessary suffering. To end devastation before it gets worse. To show compassion even in competition.

That's exactly what happened in Nineveh. When Jonah was drowning (Day 20), he cried out and God relented. He sent the fish to save him. Now Nineveh cries out and God relents. He doesn't destroy them.

Same God. Same mercy. God called the game before the destruction went any further. Watch what happens next.

The countdown stopped. Forty days became forever. The sentence was commuted. The city that should have been ash is breathing and alive. All because God saw them turn. This is the climax of the greatest revival in the Old Testament.

God saw their actions. That was crucial. Not just their words or feelings or rituals. God saw their actions, that they had turned from their evil ways. That's what got His attention. That's what moved His heart. God watches what you do, not just what you say.

We live in "thoughts and prayers" culture. We're sorry when caught. We claim to change, but our lives look the same. Nineveh? They didn't just say sorry; they stopped doing evil. Their repentance had legs. Actions, not words. Transformation, not just talk.

There's a theological truth we miss. God was waiting for an opportunity to grant mercy. He wanted to relent. That's who He is. He's not eager to condemn. He's eager to forgive. When He saw Nineveh repent, He granted mercy. That's what God does best. He saves, He restores, He gives second chances. He takes our judgement and turns it into grace.

Repentance matters because God already wants to show mercy. When we turn, we step into what He's ready to give. Mercy is His posture, and repentance is our response.

Live It Out:

- **Create a "mercy ruled" moment** for someone else. Find one person currently losing badly at life (struggling financially, relationally, spiritually). Step in and stop their suffering before it gets worse. Pay a bill. Show up. Be the mercy that calls the game.

- **Do one action this week** that demonstrates repentance. Not just saying sorry but actually changing behavior. Stop the habit. End the relationship. Delete the app. Let your actions speak.

- **Identify one person** you've been judging. Show them the same mercy God showed Nineveh. Not because they earned it, but because that's what mercy does.

CHAPTER 4
The Revival and the Rage

CHAPTER 4 is the most convicting chapter in the book because it reveals what was in Jonah's heart all along. He didn't run from Nineveh because he was afraid; he ran because he knew God would show them mercy, and he didn't want them to have it. This chapter uncovers a prophet who values justice more than compassion, his own reputation more than God's glory, a plant more than 120,000 souls.

This is the chapter that makes us squirm because this is the chapter where we see ourselves. Our selective mercy. Our conditional love. Our anger when God doesn't do what we think is fair.

Jonah is about to throw the biggest tantrum in Scripture, and God is about to respond with one of the most devastating questions in the Bible. Buckle up. This is going to sting.

DAY 37 ▪ The Rage Audit

Jonah was greatly displeased and became furious.
Jonah 4:1 (CSB)

THE day before, Jonah watched the greatest revival in history take place. 120,000 people came to faith. An entire empire was transformed. Mission accomplished. And Jonah's response? Fury. The very thing he was sent to go do became the thing he resented most.

Spiritual anger is being mad at God for being too good, too merciful, too forgiving to the wrong people.

Jonah was furious that God showed up as exactly who He said He'd be. And that fury diagnosed everything.

Let that absurdity hit you. God's messenger is furious about God's mission succeeding. The prophet was mad because people repented. Imagine being a doctor angry that your patient survived. Picture being a firefighter enraged that the house you were sent to did not burn down. Envision walking into a building demolition with a sledgehammer ready to swing, only to find every structure has been rebuilt and beautifully remodeled.

You remember Day 3, don't you? That was the day Jonah ran. Today we find out why. Jonah didn't flee because he was scared of Nineveh. He fled because he was afraid God would spare them.

Oh, God did spare them. God did what Jonah feared. He had mercy. Jonah became angry because God was compassionate. Nineveh wasn't just some random place that bothered him. They were the empire oppressing Israel, the people persecuting God's chosen for generations. Jonah wanted them dead. Jonah wanted judgment. He didn't want God to show compassion. His anger was tribal. He valued the lives of his people more than he valued God's character.

God saves an entire city and Jonah is filled with rage. He was *greatly displeased and became furious (CSB)*. The prophet became angry because God had compassion. Jonah's anger shows us what he worshiped: a rigid, legalistic idea of justice; his tribal loyalty; his ego; being right. The Rage Audit helps us see what you worship. Are you angry when God shows mercy to those who you think don't deserve it?

Here's why this is so devastating. Jonah was angry because he didn't understand grace and forgiveness. If you truly understand that you were dead in your sins and

God came to take the punishment you deserved, then seeing someone else get that same mercy should make you celebrate with joy, not anger. When you really get forgiveness (that you deserved Hell but because of Jesus you got Heaven), there is no way you won't rejoice when someone else gets that same pardon.

We live in a time where we have made anger feel righteous. But Jesus came to take what they deserve so they could have what they don't deserve. The mercy that Nineveh received from God is the same mercy that saved you from an eternity in hell. You didn't deserve to be rescued any more than they did. If Jesus hung beaten and bloody on a cross for the people who put Him there, then who are we to show any less compassion to anyone?

Live It Out:

- **Make a list of three people** whose salvation would actually make you uncomfortable. Be brutally honest. The racist uncle? The ex who destroyed you? The politician you despise? Now pray for their salvation every day this week.

- **Write a letter to God** confessing who you want judged instead of saved. Be honest about the people you'd rather see judged than redeemed. Then burn the letter and watch it turn to ash. That's what Jesus did with your list of sins. Let Him do the same with your list of enemies.

- **Identify one person you've completely written off spiritually**, someone you've stopped praying for because "they'll never change." Set a daily alarm titled with their name. Every time it goes off, pray, "God, save them the way you saved me."

Day 38 ▪ Mad About Mercy

*He prayed to the L*ORD*, "Please, L*ORD*, isn't this what I said while I was still in my own country? That's why I fled toward Tarshish in the first place. I knew that you are a gracious and compassionate God, slow to anger, abounding in faithful love, and one who relents from sending disaster."* Jonah 4:2 (CSB)

CANCEL culture exists because we believe some people are beyond redemption. Jonah wanted Nineveh canceled. One mistake, one bad take, one problematic past, and they're done. No grace, no comeback, no second chances. We want accountability, not mercy. But the scandal of the cross is that Jesus didn't come to cancel sinners; He came to save them.

Jonah's fury from yesterday wasn't just emotion. It was theology. In this prayer, he finally tells God exactly why he's so angry. Turns out, Jonah knows his Bible really well. He just hates what it says about mercy.

This isn't Jonah venting to a friend. This is Jonah praying. He's bringing his anger directly to God. That's actually healthy, radical honesty with God. The problem isn't that he's angry and praying about it. The problem is what he's angry about. He's mad that God is exactly who He says He is.

He finally tells us why he ran in the first place. *"Isn't this what I said while I was still in my own country?"* (CSB) Jonah's basically saying, "I told you so." He predicted this outcome perfectly. He knew if he preached, they'd repent. He knew if they repented, God would forgive. And he hated that. Jonah was right about God's character but wrong about what that character should mean. He knew the truth. He just hated its implications.

Then he quotes God's own words back to Him. *"Gracious and compassionate God, slow to anger, abounding in faithful love, and one who relents from sending disaster"* *(CSB).* This is straight from Exodus 34:6-7. The foundational description of God's character. Jonah knew it and could recite it perfectly. But instead of celebrating it, he weaponized it. He turned God's self-revelation into a complaint. He used God's own words as evidence against Him. That's what happens when you know the truth but refuse to apply it consistently.

The very qualities that saved Jonah (grace, compassion, slowness to anger, faithful love) are the qualities he's mad about when they're extended to others. He wanted mercy for himself but judgment for Nineveh. That's not theology. That's tribalism dressed up in religious language.

We praise God for His mercy when we are on the receiving end of it. We thank Him for His compassion when we are in need. We applaud His slowness to anger when we are the ones who did wrong. But when it's offered to our enemies? To those who have wronged us? To those we deem inferior to us? Suddenly we crave justice. Suddenly mercy is evil. We pick and choose which attributes of God we will accept.

This is the gospel exposing our cherry-picking theology. Jonah knew God's character perfectly. He just refused to apply it consistently. He picked the parts of God's nature that benefited him and complained about the parts that challenged him. That's what we do when we celebrate grace for ourselves but demand justice for others. We're not defending theology. We're defending our tribe. And Jesus didn't die on a cross to save only the people we approve of.

Live It Out:
- **Identify one person whose blessing makes you bitter.** Write down three ways God has shown them the same grace He's shown you. Force yourself to see the consistency.
- **Journal this question: "What truth do I love for me but hate for others?"** Be brutally honest. Then ask God to make you consistent in how you apply His character.
- **Read Psalm 103** slowly this week and let David's celebration of God's mercy reshape how you see who deserves it.

DAY 39 ▪ I'm Done

Now, LORD, take away my life, for it is better for me to die than to live." Jonah 4:3 (NIV)

I'M DONE. That's Jonah's response to God's grace. Not frustration. Not even anger. A death wish. *"Take away my life, for it is better for me to die than to live" (NIV).* He would rather die than see his enemies receive God's mercy. Jonah is that angry at grace.

Consider what the prophet is asking God to do. "God, you just spared 120,000 people. Kill me now." He's enraged that mercy was shown. Angry to the point that he'd rather die than see the results. He's pleading with God to kill him because God showed them grace. That's beyond anger; that's desperation and pride wrapped into one thought.

God had shown them mercy (Day 36). The city was spared. Jonah was forced to watch 120,000 people rejoice in God's forgiveness while he sat in sour resentment. He had to witness their repentance, worship, and transformation. It nearly killed him.

He couldn't stand to watch grace prevail. The greatest revival in all of history had just become his greatest source of grief. Their success was breaking him. Because they were alive, he wanted to die.

We live in an "I'm done" culture. Done with this job. Done with this relationship. Done with trying. When life doesn't go our way, we rage quit. Jonah is rage quitting life itself because God didn't do what he wanted. He's taking his ball and going home, except the ball is his life, and going home means death.

That's depression. That's spiritual burnout. That's what happens when your theology and your heart are at war. Jonah knew God was merciful; he just hated it. And that internal conflict drove him to a place where he didn't want to live anymore.

Consider what has you at your worst. What bitterness are you feeding? What unforgiveness are you nursing? Is it worth your life? Is it worth your peace? Because that's what it's costing you. Jonah chose bitterness over joy, resentment over gratitude, death over life. None of it is worth it.

"I'm done" happens when you care more about what other people get than what God has given you. It happens when you're so focused on who doesn't deserve mercy that you miss the mercy you've already received.

Live It Out:

- **Recall a time when God stood with you** when you were ready to quit. Remember His patience, His grace, His refusal to give up on you. Now ask, "Who needs that same mercy from me?"

- **Release the bitterness** you're harboring that's robbing you of your joy. Confess it to God and ask Him to take it from you. Write it down as a symbol of surrender, and then burn it. Confess it to God and ask Him to take it from you.
- **Choose gratitude.** Write a list of the mercies God has shown you. Read it daily until gratitude overshadows resentment. Let thankfulness rise higher than bitterness, and watch peace return to your heart.

DAY 40 ▪ The Film Doesn't Lie

But the LORD replied, "Is it right for you to be angry?"
Jonah 4:4 (NIV)

OUR high school basketball coach made us watch film after every game. I hated it. LOATHED it. Film doesn't lie. You see everything you messed up in front of the entire team. My coach would highlight every turnover, every missed assignment, every bad decision that I thought no one else noticed. It's hard to make excuses when the footage is staring right back at you. Even though I hated watching film, those sessions made me a better player and helped our team grow.

That's what God is doing with Jonah here. He's having him watch the film. *"Is it right for you to be angry?"* *(NIV)*. One simple question. No lecture. No harsh rebuke. God is simply asking Jonah to check the tape to see what he might have missed in the moment. God is making Jonah evaluate what's really going on inside of him. And what Jonah sees isn't pretty.

The question isn't, "Are you angry?" God knows Jonah is furious. The question is, "Is it right?" Is your anger justified? Is it proportional? Is it holy? Or is it exposing something broken in you that needs to be healed? God isn't shaming the emotion. He's questioning the source. That's exactly what we need when anger overwhelms us.

Here's how to tell the difference. Righteous anger is when your heart is focused on injustice, others being hurt, God's name being dishonored. It propels you toward actions that help people. Sinful anger is when your heart is focused on your own comfort being interrupted, your expectations being unmet, your control being challenged. It propels you toward bitterness, revenge, or disengagement.

Ask yourself, "Is my anger about someone else's suffering or my own inconvenience? Am I angry because God's glory is being attacked or because my pride is being threatened? Would I still be this angry if it didn't affect me?"

Jonah's anger was all about him. He was angry that God showed mercy to people he hated. Angry that his prediction didn't come true. Angry that he looked foolish. Nothing about Jonah's anger was holy. It was all self-focus pretending to be theological concern.

Sometimes the answer is yes. Your anger is right. Sometimes injustice should make you furious. But sometimes your anger is exposing something in you that needs to change. Your entitlement. Your self-righteousness. Your need for control. Your inability to forgive.

The tape tells the truth. Running the replay is an invitation to honesty. God asks the question not to trap you but to free you. He's giving you an opportunity to see what's really on the tape, to recognize the pattern, confess it, and let Him coach you through it. The question isn't meant to shame you. It's meant to heal you.

Live It Out:

- **Watch your own movie today.** Pick one recent circumstance where you became angry and play it back honestly. What does your tape show about your heart? Were you angry about injustice or inconvenience?
- **Pick one angry thought pattern to give up today.** When it comes to mind, replace it with a truth about God's character..
- **Cut yourself off mid-rant.** The next time you find yourself venting, complaining, or raging about something, stop yourself mid-sentence. Walk away. Don't let yourself finish that thought.

DAY 41 ▪ Revenge Is a Dish Best Served Cold

Then Jonah went out to the east side of the city and made a shelter to sit under as he waited to see what would happen to the city. Jonah 4:5 (NLT)

THERE'S a certain amount of satisfaction in watching someone who wronged you get exactly what they deserve. Haven't we all felt that draw? Jonah felt it sitting outside Nineveh with his arms crossed waiting. He'd preached God's word. He then picked the best place on the hillside for a view of destruction that never came. The city had repented. But Jonah didn't want repentance. He wanted ruin.

"Revenge is a dish best served cold" means vengeance is more satisfying when you wait patiently rather than strike in the moment. That's exactly what Jonah was doing outside Nineveh. Sitting in cold judgment waiting for God to send fire and brimstone to destroy the city he hated.

As Jonah sat watching for Nineveh's destruction, he was missing God's miraculous work. He could have been celebrating the greatest revival in history, worshiping alongside thousands of transformed hearts. Instead he chose to nurse his resentment. Wasting precious time waiting for ruin while the feast of God's grace was on display all around him.

Jonah and Jesus both had a view from a hill. Jonah's view: waiting to watch enemies burn. Jesus' view: watching enemies He was about to save. From the cross Jesus could see the Roman soldiers. He could see the mocking crowd, the religious leaders who plotted His death. Yet what was His response? *'Father, forgive them, for they don't know what they're doing" (Luke 23:34, NIV).* Jonah sat in the shade hoping for fire from heaven. Jesus hung in the sun taking fire from heaven. One prophet built a shelter to watch destruction. The greater prophet became the shelter by absorbing destruction.

What outpost have you built for your own vigil of vindication? Who are you watching from your perch, waiting for them to stumble? Jonah built an actual outpost. What's yours? A tower of anger? A highlight reel of their mistakes?

God showed mercy on Nineveh when they didn't deserve it. Jonah was rescued from the stomach of a fish. Given a second chance. Forgiveness for running away. And now he's sulking outside hoping God won't give them that same mercy. We praise God when His mercy saves us from our sin. Then we rage when His mercy rescues others from theirs. We want grace for ourselves and judgment for everyone else. Stop building outposts for vindication. Start celebrating grace.

Live It Out:

- **Remember the cross.** Jesus didn't build an outpost to watch you fail. He climbed Golgotha to take your failure on Himself. Write down one way Jesus showed you mercy you didn't deserve. Then ask, "Who needs that same mercy from me?"
- **Unfollow the social media accounts** you only check to see if they're struggling. Replace them with accounts that make you thankful.
- **Pray every day this week for those who offend you.** "Jesus, you died for them just like you died for me. Help me see them the way you do." Say it until your heart starts to believe it.

Day 42 ▪ Throwing Shade

The Lord God appointed a plant, and it grew up over Jonah to provide shade for his head to save him from his distress. Jonah was exceedingly pleased with the plant.   Jonah 4:6 (CSB)

When we use the phrase "throwing shade" today, it means to disparage someone, to disrespect them or make them seem smaller than they are. It's an insult couched as a benign statement. But when God "throws shade" in Jonah 4:6, He's doing the exact opposite. God isn't throwing Jonah under the bus. He's literally providing a bush to pick Jonah up. God appoints a plant to provide Jonah with shade, to cover Jonah from the heat of the sun. When our shade highlights weakness, God's shade covers our frailty. When our shade minimizes, God's shade shelters. This is not insult; it's grace.

Jonah is sitting on a hill with his arms folded, waiting for God to light Nineveh on fire. He thinks he is going to witness 120,000 people die. He just cursed God in front of everyone for showing compassion. He is so angry over grace that death looks better than life to him. So what does God do? God flexes. But not in an attacking way. In a rescuing way. In a comforting way. In a way you do not deserve when you are at your worst.

Stop. Jonah had the largest tantrum in Scripture. He was angry. Angry enough that he let go of his mission, challenged God's character and asked to die instead of seeing mercy. And God's response to that? Comfort rather than correction, at least not yet. Not condemnation. God ministers to Jonah, gives him relief in the middle of his rebellion. That is the scandal of grace.

This plant is every undeserved covering you've ever received: the job you didn't deserve when your résumé wasn't good enough, the relationship that didn't end when your behavior should have sent it packing, the breath in your lungs this morning when yesterday you were cursing His name.

The shade isn't comfort; it's relationship. God could have let Jonah suffer in the sun of his own wrath, but He hovered close enough to let Jonah cool off. Even in your very worst moment, He's throwing shade on you.

Ultimately God did this through Jesus. While Jonah sat under temporary shade, Jesus became our permanent covering. He sat in the heat of God's wrath on the cross so we could sit in His shade forever. While Jonah deserved exposure, God gave him covering. While we deserve judgement, Jesus took it.

The question is, will you receive it? Or are you going to continue sitting in your anger, resenting the shade that He's throwing?

Live It Out:

- **Remember a time** God threw protective shade on you when you deserved exposure. Thank Him for covering instead of condemning.

- **Pray for someone who needs God's shade** but you think deserves the heat. Ask God to cover them anyway, just like He covered Jonah when he didn't deserve it.

- **Share how God has thrown shade on your life**—the protective, gracious kind that saved you when you were at your worst.

DAY 43 · The Worm Entered the Chat

When dawn came the next day, God appointed a worm that attacked the plant, and it withered.   Jonah 4:7 (CSB)

JUST when Jonah was comfortable, God sent a worm. One worm. One appointed worm. And it destroyed the plant that made Jonah so happy. The shade was gone, the comfort was over, and Jonah was about to learn that nothing in this life is guaranteed except God's sovereignty.

When dawn came the next day (CSB). Jonah had one night of comfort. One evening of shade. One moment of being pleased. And then morning came and everything changed. That's how quickly circumstances can shift. That's how temporary earthly blessings are. What you're celebrating today might be gone tomorrow.

You know that feeling when your phone dies right before you need it? When the relationship you thought was solid suddenly ends? When the job you counted on falls through? The worm enters the chat and everything you were building your security on withers. Your loss exposes your response. Do you rage? Do you spiral? Do you blame God? Loss does not create character; it reveals it.

Jonah was so focused on the plant that he missed the lesson. He cared more about the shade than about what the shade was meant to reveal about his heart. Sometimes God removes blessings to expose priorities. Sometimes He takes away comfort to address character. Sometimes He sends a worm to show you where your treasure really is.

Yesterday, God gave Jonah shade he didn't deserve. Today, He's taking it away. Why? Because the point was never the plant. The point was teaching Jonah that God is sovereign over comfort and discomfort, blessing and loss, shade and heat. Jonah's response to losing the plant would expose what he really cared about.

That's the real test. Not what you have, but how you handle losing it. Not what God gives, but how you react when He takes it away.

Jesus lost everything so you could have everything that matters. Stripped of comfort, dignity, life itself. But He did it willingly so that when you lose what you're clinging to, you'll discover you haven't lost what matters most. You still have Him. And He's enough, even when the worm comes calling.

Live It Out:

- **Name one thing God has removed from your life that you're still bitter about.** Ask Him what He was trying to teach you through it. Listen for His answer.

- **Thank God for His sovereignty even in the losses.** Even when the worm enters the chat. Even when comfort gets destroyed. Worship Him anyway.

- **Examine your response to loss.** Does losing things reveal entitlement, bitterness, or dependence on temporary comforts? Confess what needs confessing. Change what needs changing.

DAY 44 ▪ You're Not the Boss of Me

As the sun was rising, God appointed a scorching east wind. The sun beat down on Jonah's head so much that he almost fainted, and he wanted to die. Jonah 4:8 (CSB)

ALL control freaks get their reckoning eventually. Jonah got his when God tore his cushy bubble apart. First the plant. Then the shade. Now, scorching wind and blazing sun. God had to smash Jonah's life to bits to get his attention.

As the sun was rising, God appointed a scorching east wind. (CSB). God sends a blast of hot wind and sun. Jonah goes from cocooned comfort to miserable agony in less than 24 hours. This isn't just a heat wave. This is God giving Jonah a masterclass in sovereignty.

Notice the pattern. God appointed the fish to save Jonah. God appointed the plant to comfort him. God appointed the worm to strip his comfort away. Now God appoints a scorching wind to expose him. Every single detail is under God's sovereign appointment. Nothing is left to chance. And Jonah has zero control over any of it.

All of us have been there. The meltdown when a delayed flight blows up your plans. The downward spiral when someone else gets the promotion. The tantrum when your timeline hits a snag. The bitterness when God won't give you what you want when you want it. We're just like Jonah. "I'd rather die than accept the fact that this isn't going my way."

Jonah's death wish wasn't really about the plant or the heat. It was about pride. About ego. About wanting his own way. About refusing to accept God's sovereign rule over his comfort, his mission, his expectations, his enemies. Better to die than submit. He was so proud he nearly died.

Contrast Jonah to Jesus. Jonah says, "I'd rather die than submit." Jesus says, "Not my will but yours" and dies submitting to the Father. One flawed prophet battled God's sovereignty until he was about to faint from exhaustion. The perfect Prophet surrendered totally, and in that surrender redeemed the world.

The question isn't whether God is in control. He is. The question is whether you will battle it until you nearly faint from exhaustion, or bow the knee and finally submit. One path leads to death wishes. The other to peace.

Live It Out:

- **Pray Jesus' prayer** in Gethsemane over one area you are trying to control. Say it out loud: "Not my will, but yours be done in [specific situation]."

Repeat it every morning this week until surrender is your default and resistance is the exception.

- **Identify one "appointment"** from God you have been resisting/fighting (job loss, move, relationship ended, closed door). Write it down. Next to it write, "God appointed this. Jesus, teach me to surrender like you did." Post it where you will see it every day.

- **Confess to God your need to be in control.** Ask Him to help you trust His appointments even when they are not what you would like. Pray for a heart of submission.

Day 45 ▪ Comfort Wars

But God said to Jonah, "Is it right for you to be angry about the plant?" "It is," he said. "And I'm so angry I wish I were dead." Jonah 4:9 (NIV)

THE AC breaks on the hottest day of summer. No one can fix it for five days. You're sweating, uncomfortable, unable to sleep. You text, "I literally can't live like this." Meanwhile, your neighbor just lost their job. Your coworker's marriage is falling apart. A friend texted asking for prayer and you still haven't responded. Right now, all you can think about is your personal comfort.

This is exactly what happened to Jonah. God asked, "Do you have a right to be angry?" Jonah answered, "Yes, I have a right to be angry enough to die!" He's doubling down. Protecting his comfort. Rationalizing his fit because of a plant that lived for one day. A plant he didn't plant, didn't water, didn't deserve. And while

120,000 people just came to God, Jonah couldn't have cared less.

That is heartbreaking. Jonah valued his comfort more than eternal lives. Let's hold Jonah accountable before we realize we fight the same fight.

Jonah's disproportionate anger points us to the disease of the heart: entitlement. "I deserve comfort. I deserve control. I deserve better than this." When you rage over small things, you're not really upset about the situation. You're upset that reality refused to cater to your preferences.

Welcome to the Comfort Wars. This is the battle we wage daily: what we want vs. what God wants, our preferences vs. His purposes, personal ease vs. Kingdom priorities. Jonah declared war over a plant. We declare war over parking spots, Wi-Fi speed, room temperature.

Think about the difference between Jonah and Jesus. It should crush us. Jonah sulks with a death wish because he didn't get some shade. Jesus accepts the cross without complaint for undeserving sinners. One gets angry because he lost comfort. The other gave up everything to provide comfort.

When minor inconveniences produce major rage, something's wrong internally, not externally. The problem isn't the situation. It's your soul. Jesus modeled the opposite of entitlement. He had every right to comfort, yet He chose the cross. He deserved worship, yet He served. That's what surrender looks like. Not getting what you want but choosing joy anyway.

Live It Out:

- **Ask yourself honestly,** "What am I most angry about right now?" Write it down. Then ask, "Do I have a right to be angry about this?" Answer truthfully. Let the question expose your entitlement.

- **Identify one area where your anger** is clearly disproportionate to the situation. Confess it to God. Ask Him to restore your perspective and replace your entitlement with surrender.

- **Pray this prayer daily:** "Jesus, you gave up everything you deserved so I could have everything I don't deserve. Forgive my entitlement. Replace it with surrender. Help me care more about what you care about than my own comfort." Mean it.

DAY 46 ▪ The Mic Drop

Then the LORD said, "You feel sorry about the plant, though you did nothing to put it there. It came quickly and died quickly. But Nineveh has more than 120,000 people living in spiritual darkness, not to mention all the animals. Shouldn't I feel sorry for such a great city?" Jonah 4:10-11 (NLT)

THE Book of Jonah ends not with a bang but with the most uncomfortable question in all of Scripture. It's not, "How could God forgive Nineveh?" but, "How could you not want Him to?" God drops the mic and walks away, leaving Jonah (and us) to sit with the silence of this question we'd rather not answer.

God shines a spotlight on Jonah's ridiculousness that he cared nothing about a plant that lived 24 hours, but mourned its death more than he celebrated over 120,000 people being spared. Plant vs. people. Shade vs. souls. Comfort vs. compassion. God says these Ninevites are spiritual prostitutes, morally bankrupt, and don't know any better. God loves them anyway.

This is the point Jonah drives home about what hinders revival in our hearts. We scroll past human tragedy but lose our minds over our Starbucks running out of Wi-Fi. We care more about our convenience than the people God invented a passion for. True revival doesn't bypass this. When God shakes things up in power, He doesn't only work on the unsaved, He'll work on the "saved" too. Revival will show us if we want what God wants or if we just want God to bless what we want. Jonah wanted revival with stipulations: death for his enemies. God wanted revival without restrictions: mercy for sinners, transformation for the worst of societies.

But Jonah's story points to something greater. God asked, "Shouldn't I feel sorry for Nineveh?" The book ends with God's question hanging in the balance. We never learn how Jonah answered, and that's intentional because your story is still being written. The question isn't whether Jonah changed; it's whether we will. Will you care about what God cares about? Will you value people over preferences, souls over comfort, God's compassion over your convenience?

Stop caring more about your comfort than God's compassion. Let His heart for lost people become the driving force behind your witness and prayers.

Live It Out:

- **Examine Your Priorities:** Identify three things you care more about than the eternal destiny of lost people, and ask God to reorder your heart.

- **Develop God's Heart:** Volunteer with a ministry that serves people who are far from God, asking Him to give you His compassion for those who are spiritually lost.
- **Answer the Question:** Spend extended time in prayer this week honestly answering God's question, "May I not care about lost people?" and let that truth shape how you live.

DAY 47 ▪ Greater than Jonah

"For just as Jonah was three days and three nights in the belly of the great fish, so the Son of Man will be three days and three nights in the heart of the earth." Matthew 12:40 (CSB)

YOU'VE tracked with a prophet who ran, raged, and reluctantly obeyed. You didn't quit when it got uncomfortable. You stayed when Jonah's heart looked too much like yours. Now there's one more thing you need to see.

Jesus said the story of Jonah was about Him. When religious leaders demanded proof that He was the Messiah, Jesus pointed to Jonah's three days in the fish. They wanted a sign. Jesus gave them the greatest sign in history: Himself.

Do you see the pattern? Jonah went down into death, spent three days in darkness, came back to life, and then preached to Gentiles who desperately needed mercy. Jesus did the exact same thing, but infinitely greater. Death on the cross, three days in the tomb, resurrection on the third day, and then the gospel going out to all nations. Jonah previewed it. Jesus fulfilled it.

Jonah was rescued from death so he could finish his mission. Jesus conquered death so you could have eternal life. Jonah's sign saved one generation in one city. Jesus' resurrection offers salvation to anyone who believes, anywhere, at any time, forever.

Just as Jonah and Jesus both overcame death on the third day, God wants you to have a resurrected life too. Not just someday in eternity, but right now. Dead to sin. Alive to God. A life transformed by the same power that raised Jesus from the grave.

Jonah ran from his calling. Jesus ran toward the cross. Jonah preached judgment. Jesus absorbed the judgment and offers you grace. Jonah was furious when mercy won. Jesus rejoiced when sinners were saved. Jonah was the preview. Jesus is the reality.

Have you surrendered your life to this greater-than-Jonah Savior? You're like Nineveh, spiritually lost without Him. You're like Jonah, running and caring more about comfort than souls. Jesus died for you and rose to give you the life you couldn't earn.

If you've never trusted Jesus, today's the day. Confess that you need Him. Believe He died for you and rose again. Surrender your life to Him as Lord. Repent. Believe. Follow.

If you know Jesus, Nineveh received mercy because one reluctant prophet finally obeyed. How many people around you are spiritually lost, waiting for someone to tell them about Jesus? God pursued Jonah so Jonah could pursue Nineveh. Jesus pursued you so you could pursue your Nineveh.

Live like it. Love like it. Tell others about it. Your Nineveh is waiting.

Live It Out:

- **Write yourself a letter describing who you were on Day 1 and who you are now.** Seal it. Open it in six months and see what Jesus has done.

- **Text someone today, "I just finished reading Jonah.** May I tell you what I learned about Jesus?" And then tell them.

- **Read through Jonah one more time this week.** See how differently you read it now. Let everything you've learned change how you view God's gracious mercy.

CONCLUSION
Revival Ready

THROUGHOUT this journey, we've watched a reluctant prophet run from mercy, rage against it, and resent it. You've seen God pursue, rescue, and use someone who spent most of the book fighting Him. You've walked through three revivals in four chapters: sailors on a ship, a prophet in a fish, sinners in a city.

But don't overlook that you're part of this story too. The same God who revived a ship full of sailors, a drowning prophet, and a city full of sinners is still in the revival business and is still pursuing people. He is still rescuing rebels. Still extending mercy to those who don't deserve it. Still turning the most unlikely people into His instruments of grace. Still using reluctant prophets who finally stop running and say yes to a relentless God.

Our great ambition is that God would do in our generation what He did in Jonah's. That He would bring personal revival to hearts that have grown cold. That He would spark spiritual awakening in cities that seem beyond hope. That He would use reluctant, flawed, ordinary people like us to carry His message to a world that desperately needs to hear it.

Our goal is for God to use us the way He used Jonah. Not because we're qualified. Not because we have it all together. Not because our hearts are pure and our motives are perfect. But because we're willing. Because we've stopped running. Because we've experienced His mercy and we can't keep it to ourselves. Because we've let these 47 days make us revival ready.

Jonah teaches us that before God can use you to bring revival to others, He has to bring revival to you first. He has to get your heart ready. That's what the fish was for Jonah. That's what these chapters have been for you. God has been preparing you, reshaping you, stripping away everything that would keep you from caring about what He cares about. He's been getting your heart ready to be used.

The question isn't whether God can bring revival. Jonah's story proves He can. The question is whether you're revival ready. Whether you'll go to your Nineveh. Whether you'll care about what God cares about. Whether you'll let His relentless mercy change not just your story but the stories of everyone around you.

Jonah's story ended with a question from God that's been hanging in the air for 2,800 years. But your story doesn't have to end there. You can answer it. You can live it. You can watch what happens when reluctant prophets finally say yes to a relentless God.

Your Nineveh is waiting. You're revival ready. Go.

TOPIC INDEX

ALL RESOURCES ON RYANHELLER.ORG
LIVE BOLD
with RYAN & GENA HELLER

GOD
Do All Religions Lea
The Same God?
THE REAL JESUS?

SUBSCRIBE TO RYAN
HELLER MINISTRIES ON

FOR MORE RESOURCES FROM RYAN HELLER GO TO

RYANHELLER.ORG

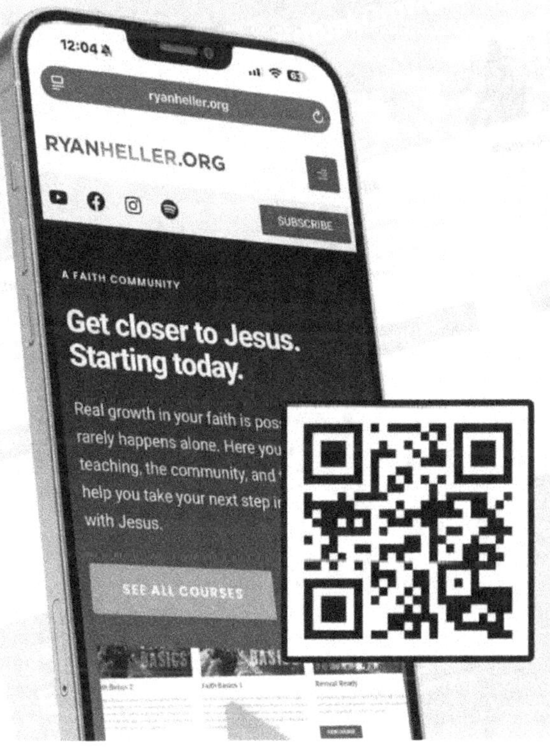

www.ingramcontent.com/pod-product-compliance
Lightning Source LLC
Chambersburg PA
CBHW071346150726
47997CB00002B/866